FREE TO CHOOSE

Youth Program Resource from the Black Experience

Mary Adebonojo

Judson Press ® Valley Forge

8780 Free To Choose
Free to Choose

Copyright © 1980
The Executive Council of the Episcopal Church, Commission on Black
Ministry

Second Printing, 1980

Unless otherwise indicated, Bible quotations in this volume are from *The
Holy Bible,* King James Version.

Other quotations of the Bible are from the Revised Standard Version of the
Bible, copyrighted 1946, 1952, 1971, 1973 © by the Division of Christian
Education of the National Council of the Churches of Christ in the United
States of America, and are used by permission.

Library of Congress Cataloging in Publication Data

Adebonojo, Mary.
　　Free to choose.

　　1. Christian education of young people.
　　2. Afro-American youth—Religious life. I. Title.
BV1485.A3　　268'.433　　79-26705
ISBN 0-8170-0853-5

The name JUDSON PRESS is registered as a trademark in the U.S. Patent
Office.
Printed in the U.S.A. ✛

The photographs on pages 4, 10, 18, 33, 49, 54, 66, 78, 108, 120, and 137 are
copyrighted by Ed Eckstein

Foreword

This curriculum resource was developed in response to the many requests received for Christian education materials particularly appropriate for black Christians. It also grew out of a black theological perspective.

Those of us in predominantly white denominations and ethnically mixed congregations can especially benefit from this resource. So often the materials available to us are written from a white Christian perspective and therefore neither take into account nor address the peculiar experiences of black and other ethnic peoples.

Therefore, this effort is an attempt by the Commission for Black Ministries of the Episcopal Church to provide materials grounded in the Christian tradition which deal with themes and issues confronted by blacks historically as well as in their contemporary experiences.

Moreover, this resource book carries out the recommendation of the Theological Purpose/Programmatic Statement developed and published by the Commission for Black Ministries. The Statement also suggested that a hymnal of Negro spirituals and other songs be developed as a worship resource.

All of these materials are designed to help blacks and others learn, worship, and experience the Christian faith in their own cultural context. It is also hoped that these materials will help others understand and appreciate the milieu in which blacks live, move, and have their being.

Obviously, this resource curriculum has involved the hard work and participation of many people, especially those at Saint Barnabas Episcopal Church and the Church of the Advocate in Philadelphia, Pennsylvania, where the project was based.

A great deal of credit must go to the Reverend Mary Adebonojo, project director and writer, and her staff for an excellent job. Elyse V. Bradt served as research and administrative assistant; Leslie Grady and Renee Jones, writers; Nellie Parker and Margaret Rice, consultants for testing; Marjorie Thomas, coordinator for white congregations; Edward Thomas, treasurer of the project; and Rosalie Lloyd and Gladys Underwood, typists. Thanks are also due to the Reverend Richard Tolliver for his editorial help and his aid with training sessions for the material in this book.

The Office of Religious Education of the Episcopal Church fully supported and cooperated in the development of this enterprise and endorses its use in our congregations.

The Commission for Black Ministries thinks this book is a valuable resource and hopes it will be widely used throughout the church.

We commend it to clergy, church educators, church school teachers, and church groups for use in their educational program.

The Reverend Franklin D. Turner, D.D.
Staff Officer for Black Ministries
Episcopal Church Center
New York, New York

Contents

Introduction

Free to Choose is a resource designed to enable black American youth between the ages of eleven and eighteen to reflect on their history and life experiences in the light of their Christian faith. It is suitable for use as an alternative for church school, for vacation Bible school, for youth and fellowship groups, for retreats and conferences, and for midweek activity programs. Although especially designed for older children and youth, most of the sessions, long-term projects, and retreats can also be used with adult groups, and many are appropriate for intergenerational family night programs as well. *Free to Choose* is also an important resource for nonblack and mixed congregations who wish to explore some of the particular needs and concerns of the black community or develop a greater understanding of a black perspective. Moreover, the instructional method which is used in the long-term projects in this book and which is explained in detail in Appendix A can be of general use with Christians of any race. Hispanic, Native American, and other peoples living in American inner-city neighborhoods may also find this resource helpful. Although all illustrations and examples are drawn from the black experience, the topics chosen for discussion and the perspective from which these topics are viewed may well be familiar to these groups, too.

Most of the sessions in the resource are designed to last about one to one and a half hours and use materials which usually are available in the church school. Each session is complete in itself; outlines include both content and process, with summaries of any necessary background material. Most require about twenty-five minutes preparation if the adult leader chooses not to share the planning, session leadership, or evaluation with the youth. But nearly all of the planning, leadership, and evaluation of the sessions can be done by the youth themselves, with some guidance. The members of the group or a smaller planning committee can decide which sessions they would like to use and when. They can also divide up the responsibility for presenting the session as each of the leaders for the day, perhaps, prepares and leads one step in the session with the group. Evaluation, then, which can also be carried out with the group (see Appendix E), would not only enable the leaders to determine how effectively they led the session but would also be invaluable for determining what kinds of sessions to use with the group in the future.

Some sessions are labeled "with a little planning." These usually involve an event which requires some advance preparation or the use of materials or equipment which are not generally available in church school. Leaders will find, also, that while some session outlines have full directions and even the expected answers given in parentheses, others give greater scope for individualized input and creative planning. It will be best for the leader to put into his or her own words the material within quotation marks throughout the book. If necessary, however, the material can be read to the group.

The following is a breakdown by session of the various kinds of vehicles used for teaching in this book according to the degree of difficulty which a teacher might experience in using each one. Roman numerals refer to the session number of the unit.

The teacher should have no difficulty with these:

1. Role play in twos—Decision Making II, Justice III, Suffering III
2. Role play in groups: Suffering III
3. Role play where small groups instruct the players and afterward answer questions: Decision Making I, Bread I, Suffering III
4. Activity for reflection: Decision Making I, Loving Ourselves II
5. Open-ended stories, case histories, multiple-ending stories: Faith I, Justice II, Suffering I, II
6. Game introducing content: Faith I; Black Men, Black Women I

7. Simulation game: Decision Making IV, Values II
8. Activities:
   Decision Making I (comics and posters)
   Justice IV (invitations and posters)
   Bread I (Help Wanted Board)
   Bread II, Community IV (relating board)
   Suffering II (respond board)
   Suffering IV (intercession notebook)
   Suffering I (intercession board)
9. Litanies: Black Men, Black Women I; Faith I
10. Round Robin prayers: Suffering IV, Community IV
11. Groups empathizing with a Bible character: Faith III, Suffering II
12. Image prayers: Values III, Faith II, Decision Making II, III, Community III
13. Biblical summaries: Values III; Black Men, Black Women I; Community IV; Faith I; Decision Making I; Community III; Suffering II
14. Survey, observation, canvass: Community III, Suffering IV, Bread II

The teacher may experience a moderate degree of difficulty with these:
1. Activities:
   Faith I (collage)
   Values III (collage)
   Faith II (costumes and scenery)
   Faith III (sock puppets)
   Loving Ourselves I (cardboard masks)
   Justice III (dance)
2. Banners, vestments, etc., for the religious celebration
3. Image prayers: Bread II, Decision Making I

The teacher may experience considerable difficulty with these:
1. Small-group discussions, visioning, force-field analysis, etc.: Faith II, Suffering IV, Community I, II, III, IV, Values I, Justice I, II, III, IV, Decision Making II, III
2. Creative Drama: Faith II, Community I
3. African folk material (a cassette recording which will help with this material can be obtained from the Office for Black Ministries, Episcopal Church Center, 815 Second Avenue, New York, NY 10017): Justice I; Values I; Black Men, Black Women I
4. Planning with the youth, dividing session leadership among the youth, and evaluating with the youth
5. Planning the corporate social action project

It is clear that the particular subjects presented in this book reflect some of the interests, needs, and concerns of black people and the questions raised in their daily existence. In addition, these interests, needs, and concerns are presented from the perspective from which black people view them. Illustrations for these subjects are drawn from black history integrated with social and cultural experiences from African folklore. However, African and Afro-American history and culture are not used for their own sake. Rather, they are utilized to facilitate focusing on the question "What is it to be a black Christian?" which is the major concern of this book. Although what it is to be a black Christian is an evolving phenomenon (and especially so for blacks in predominantly white denominations), uniquely black ways of doing Christianity should have some place here. Thus, black stylistic preferences were a consideration in putting together the resources. Most of the suggestions for music in the sessions are selected from hymns and spirituals which have been used and loved by blacks, in many cases, for a long period of time. Since the black church delights in the use of symbolism, a fair amount of symbolism is included. And the stately cadences of the King James Version of the Bible (which for many blacks is still *the* Bible) are used in most places where biblical quotations are used.

Processes which are familiar to the African or black American way of life are also employed. For instance, traditional African folklore was often used for teaching, just as it is used here for that purpose. And since in the historic black American religious tradition everything is referred to Jesus, prayer or meditation, often specifically in the presence of Christ, is a part of the process in every session. Thus, both content and process participate to some extent in teaching what it is to be a black Christian and, more generally, what it is to be a Christian.

If being a Christian includes action as well as worship and is, in fact, a never-ending learning process, it stands to reason that we must take process seriously as a vehicle for teaching. Thus, an attempt has been made in this resource to integrate learning and doing and being and becoming; to use both content and process as means of instruction; and to include various levels of human experience—cognitive, affective, physical, and behavioral. In this way it is hoped that the whole person will be involved in the experience.

Perhaps the attempt to use process as a teaching tool is most obvious in the six units which provide outlines and suggestions for a long-term project. The long-term project provides an opportunity for study, research, prayer, worship, and corporate action on a theme or topic and is intended to illustrate how these various parts of the faith experience can be meaningfully and purposefully related to one another in the life of the Christian. Thus, the process used in these outlines can readily be used by the youth as a model for inquiry and action in their personal religious life.

As Christians, we are called primarily to respond to God's self-revelation as well as that which is revealed to us concerning God's will for us as God's people. For us, both the revelation and the response seen in Christ Jesus are definitive. The Christ event, on the one hand, reveals to us more fully than any other event the nature of God and of the divine will for us. On the other hand, we see in Christ what the optimal human response should be. Our task as Christians is to respond ever more fully to God's grace so that in every area of our individual and corporate lives we approach more closely the total response Christ made. As together in and with Christ we respond to God's grace, we as the Body of Christ work with Christ, our Head, to bring all things into conformity with God's will. The long-term project works entirely within this context of revelation and response to form the basis of a purposeful and meaningful Christian way of life.

Each project begins with a commitment service— which may be a corporate communion—where members of the group covenant with God and one another to pursue this topic together. Then the group uses all or any of the sessions in the unit, plus study, prayer, and research on the topic, culminating in planning some appropriate corporate social action; this planning includes discussion of any negative aspects of the action project which can be anticipated. Home devotions are planned on the theme, and, finally, the group participates in a religious celebration (Holy Communion, the Eucharist, etc.). The first part of the service, as it is sketched in Appendix J, gives the biblical and theological background concerning the topic; the Communion provides an opportunity for the group members to offer themselves and the corporate action they have planned in union with Christ's offering of himself. After the service, the group works to carry out the social action it has planned, continuing with daily prayer based on the theme of the unit. Finally, there is evaluation of the entire experience. Part of the long-term project outline can effectively be carried out on weekend conferences or retreats. A more detailed presentation of this process is given in Appendix A.

I would like to encourage the use of the long-term option in the book. However, many teachers may shy away from using it because the long-term outlines seem to give less direction and less support to the teacher than the single-session outlines do. It is through using these outlines, though, that youth can come to see study, research, prayer, and social action all as possible responses to God's revelation, as a kind of worship which is clarified and focused in the formal worship services of the church, and as means of putting into action the prayer "Thy kingdom come, Thy will be done."

The logical final step for the long-term project is not written yet. It is not written because it should be written, or more properly, carried out, at the local level. The final step would involve groups at the local level in making an analysis of the problems they face in their particular situations. Then, after searching out, meditating upon, and interpreting the relevant parts of the revelation (with the help of someone with theological training), they would determine the various responses which they should make as black people of God in that place. Thus, the youth will, in a way that is particularly suited to themselves, learn to be and become who they are called to be—the church, the Body of Christ, joined with Christ to carry out his work in the world.

Unit on Decision Making

Background

1

Decision making is an especially important topic for us as blacks. Since God makes choices and we are all, as human beings, made in God's image, God expects us to make choices, too. However, certain human conditions, such as slavery, have at times imposed severe limitations on our ability to make the decisions which affect our lives. Session I in this unit allows the youth to look at decision making under slavery.

Although as black people in the United States we are no longer slaves or hampered by legal segregation in making choices, other conditions and habits often prevent us from making wise decisions based on an appraisal of a wide range of options or alternative solutions. Session II and IV show what happens when one makes decisions based on a limited range of alternatives. Sessions I and II introduce a decision-making, problem-solving procedure and facilitate discussion of Christian goals and values in decision making. In Session III the youth try out procedures to determine whether or not one can reach a set goal and what to do if the goal does not seem to be immediately attainable. The suggested long-term projects for this unit give the youth an opportunity to explore some of the options and alternatives open to them in areas where, as teenagers or preteens, they will soon be called on to make decisions.

We Are Free to Choose

PURPOSE

To enable youth

—to know that God wants us to make choices

—to see the limitations imposed on decision making during slavery

—to see a decision-making, problem-solving model

—to see the goals and values important for Christians in decision making

—to experience how it felt to be a slave

—to experience how it feels to confront a problem or decision

—to experience how it feels to have Christ with us in decision making

OUTLINE OF SESSION

Step 1— Compasses Are Nice, But God Wants Us to Choose

Step 2— Choice in Chains

Step 3— It's Hard to Choose

Step 4— Trying Out Choice

Step 5— Prayer: Choosing with Christ

Step 6— Song

Step 7— Activity: Is That What You Would Choose to Do? Which Do You Choose?

(Step 8—Evaluation)

Step 1—Compasses Are Nice, But God Wants Us to Choose

Note: Leaders of older youth groups may skip 1, 2, and 3 below and begin in 4 at the sentence "As people, we are made in the image of God."

1. Bring a small compass to the session, and have the members of the group look at it.

2. Ask several of the youth to walk in different directions in the room, carrying the compass.

3. Then ask: "Which direction does the compass needle always point?" (north)

4. Comment: "Compasses are useful in helping us find directions because no matter whether we go north or south or east or west, the compass needle always points north. The compass needle cannot choose to point in any other direction. But people are very different from compasses. As people, we are made in the image of God (see Genesis 1:26). We know that God makes choices. God chose the Israelites as a special people. God chose to send Jesus Christ to earth. Because we are made in God's image, God expects us to choose, too. Through Joshua God told the Israelite people to choose whether they would serve the one true

God or some other god (Joshua 24:15). Before Joshua demanded that the people choose, he told the people both what God had done for them in the past and what the consequences would be if they did not serve God properly in the future (Joshua 24:1-20). Joshua wanted the people to be able to make a wise decision based on all the facts.

"God still wants us to make wise decisions. Today we are going to look at the question of choice. We are going to look at what choice meant for people in slavery, as our people were years ago, and what choice means for us as a free people."

Step 2—Choice in Chains

1. Divide the youth into two groups.

2. Give or tell each of the groups one of the situations printed below.

3. Ask each group to decide what would happen as a result of the decision made in the situation.

4. Read Situation #1 aloud. Then ask the group that discussed Situation #1 to act out both the situation and what they think would have happened as a result of the decision made in the situation.

Note: Leaders of older youth may simply ask each group to explain to the others what they think might have happened as a result of the decision made.

5. Ask the members of the other group to explain why they agree or disagree with the result Group #1 presented.

6. Repeat 4 and 5 above for Group #2 with Situation #2.

Situation #1

The Israelite people are slaves in Egypt. The Pharaoh, or king, of Egypt has forced the Israelites to build great buildings for Egypt. He is anxious that the buildings be finished soon. He has a large and powerful army. The Israelites want to go into the desert for several days to worship their God. The Pharaoh refuses to allow them to leave. What would happen if they simply walked off as a body into the desert?

Situation #2

Leroy is a black slave in America. He works in the fields. The master of the plantation where Leroy is a slave is afraid that the crop will not be harvested before the rains come. He has given his slave drivers whips and instructed them to be sure that the slaves are kept working all the time. Leroy is very tired. What do you think would happen if he decides to sit down in the shade for a few minutes?

7. Ask both groups: "How would you feel if you could not decide to worship God as you pleased? How would you feel if you knew that you would not receive any money for the work you had done but could not decide to stop working to rest when you were tired?" (Angry, sad, unhappy?)

8. Comment: "Although slaves in different places in the world have been treated differently, slaves generally were not able to make many decisions for themselves. And it is often difficult for people to live happily under such conditions. Now that we are a free people and especially as you become adults, there are many decisions to be made. As you will see, though, it is not always easy to make decisions."

Step 3—It's Hard to Choose

Note: Leaders of older youth may skip the "Dumb School" game and begin with the commentary, "Often, we don't know which way to choose. . . ."

Arrange the chairs in rows. Ask each of the two groups from Step 2 to play two or three rounds of "Dumb School." (In "Dumb School" one person, the leader, stands before the group, secretly hides an object in either hand, and asks each member of the group to decide which of his or her outstretched closed hands holds the object. The person deciding indicates his or her choice by tapping the hand which he or she thinks holds the object. If the choice is correct, the one who chose moves to the next "grade" [row of chairs]. Before moving to the next participant, the leader again hides the object in one hand or the other.)

After the game ask: "Was it easy to decide which hand to choose? Were you afraid that you might make a mistake?" Then give this commentary:

"Making choices is sometimes not easy. Often, we don't know which way to choose and are afraid that we might make a mistake. There are many procedures devised to help people solve their problems and make decisions. One of these procedures suggests that when making a decision, you (1) look at the GOAL you want to reach; (2) consider your VALUES, the things that are important to you; (3) consider the facts in the situations and the different options or ALTERNATIVES that you could choose; (4) consider the possible CONSEQUENCES for each alternative—what would happen as a result of choosing that alternative; and (5) consider whether or not you could live with the probable consequences of the alternative upon which you have decided.

"For Christians, the Bible also gives guidance for making decisions. We already know what goals and values are most important as we go about making decisions as Christians. We know that we must be like God, that we must be holy, as God is holy (1 Peter 1:15-16). We know that "God is love" (1 John 4:16), and Jesus tells us to love God with all our heart, soul, and mind, and our neighbor as ourselves (Matthew 22:37, 39). Thus, the goal of every decision for a Christian should be to do what is most loving, and the most important values are those such as compassion, respect, and truthfulness—values which normally express love. In looking at alternatives in solving a problem or making a decision, the Christian is called on to choose the one which best expresses love in the situation.

"Even with these guidelines, however, it isn't always easy to make a decision as a Christian. We may find it hard to live with the consequences of the alternative which our Christian faith seems to indicate is the best one. We may even find it difficult to decide which alternative in the situation is the most loving.

"Let's look at several examples, though, to see just what the decision-making process is all about."

Step 4—Trying Out Choice

1. Divide the youth into two groups.

2. Read or tell both groups one of the situations given below or in Session II, Step 3.

3. Ask the members of both groups what they think is the goal of the person who must make the decision—what he or she is trying to do or get.

4. Then ask first one group and then the other to act out the situation showing one of the possible alternatives which the person involved could have chosen as his or her decision.

Note: Older youth groups may simply discuss the various alternatives.

5. Ask "What values would have been most important to the person who made the decision if he or she chose the alternative presented by Group 1? What values were most important in choosing the alternative presented by Group 2? Which alternative best reflects Christian goals and values and why? What are the probable consequences for each of the alternatives presented?"

For example, in Situation A Martin's goal is to get the things from the store which his mother requested. It may also be his goal to try to obey his mother and stay out of fights. He will have to decide which value is more important—to try to stay out of fights or to try to get the things from the store which his mother requested. If he decides to fight Joey, it would seem that the most important value for him in this situation is to defend his property and bring home the things his mother wants from the store. It is difficult to say which is the

13

most loving and thus the most Christian decision here. While we tend to think that fighting is not loving, it is not really loving to allow others to victimize or take advantage of us either.

Situation A

Martin's mother had given him five dollars to get some things for her at the store. As he walked down the street, he turned around and saw Joey, a boy in his class, coming toward him. Joey was a bully. But though he was constantly boasting that he could beat up everyone in the class, Martin was not so sure. Since Martin's mother had told him that it was not good to fight, though, Martin had mainly avoided Joey.

When Joey reached Martin, he grabbed his arm. "OK, Martin," said Joey, "I know you've got some money in your pocket. You give it to me, or I'm going to break your arm."

Martin didn't want to give Joey his mother's money, but he didn't want to fight either. What should he do?

Situation B

Annie Mae went into the corner grocery store. Every time she went to that store, she got mad because items there were so expensive. These little stores in the ghetto were something else! Always a few cents more on everything! Well, it was still a lot closer than going eight or nine blocks to the supermarket. There used to be a supermarket in this block, but it closed down. Now there was only this "rip-off joint." Annie Mae saw the store owner down at the other end of the store talking to a little old man. So why should she wait for him? She could just put it in her pocketbook and walk out, and he'd never know the difference. Of course, that would be stealing. But why shouldn't she "liberate" a jar of hair oil? It would serve him right! He was charging too much anyway.

Annie Mae stood there undecided. What should she do?

Situation C

The bell rang for the end of class, and Jerry got up to leave the room. "Hey, man," came a voice from behind him, "I want to talk to you outside after school, man." It was Monkey. Monkey was the treasurer of the Bantus, a gang from the neighborhood where Jerry had just moved. Jerry was not surprised that Monkey had spoken to him because he had expected that the Bantus would try to recruit him. But he wasn't sure that he wanted to join.

The Bantus was a fighting gang, and to Jerry fighting gangs were scary. Shooting up other people or getting cut up was not his idea of having fun. But being a member of a gang could come in handy, too. Just

yesterday some kids had tried to shake him down for money on his way to school. If he decided not to join the Bantus, he would probably be beaten up anyway. Last week when two boys refused to join the Bantus, they were badly beaten. Monkey and his boys would expect an answer after school. What should he do?

Step 5—Prayer: Choosing with Christ

Place in front of the group the meditation picture for this session, found in Appendix B. (The meditation picture shows a Y-shaped, lonely, dirt road. There are no houses along the road. The two ends of the road at the top are obscured by trees, bushes, etc.) Have the members of the group focus on the picture. Ask them to think of themselves as being in the presence of God and to continue gazing at the picture throughout the meditation. Then ask the following questions, allowing enough time after each question for the youth to think it over and answer it in their minds.

1. "Suppose that you have come to the road in the picture and are seeing it for the first time. You are walking up this road, beginning from the bottom of the picture. You come to the place where the road divides. You know that the place where you want to go is at the end of one of these divisions in the road, but you don't know which one. It is very important to you that you get to your destination. There are no signs and no one around to help you make your decision. What are you thinking?

2. "How do you feel as you get to the place where the road divides?

3. "Suppose someone who is wiser and stronger than you are told you that he would help you figure out which road to take but that the final choice would be left up to you. Suppose this person said, also, that he would go along with you to help you on the way.

4. "You do have someone who will help you figure out which choice to make and who will go along with you to help you on the way. That person is Christ. Turn to him now in your mind and tell him what you are likely to be thinking and feeling when it comes time to make a choice. You just went through that process when you came in your mind to the place where the road divides. In your mind discuss with Christ your needs and fears. Tell him how knowing that he will be along on your journey makes you feel about him."

Allow the group to continue in silence for a short while. Then invite any who wish to share with the group any parts of their meditation.

Step 6—Song

Sing "Lead Me, Guide Me," "He's Got the Whole World in His Hands," "Lord, I Want to Be a Christian," or some other appropriate song.

Step 7—Activity: Is That What You Would Choose to Do? Which Do You Choose?

Have the members of the group make comic strips or posters on heavy paper or cardboard. The comic strips or posters can present a decision-making situation with one or several possible solutions and can ask either the question "Is that what you would choose to do?" or "Which do you choose?" (You may use situations outlined in Step 4 or others that are of importance to the members of the group.) Place the finished posters around the church building as a way of starting conversation between the members of the group and other members of the congregation on the subject of decision making.

(Step 8—Evaluation)

To evaluate the session with members of the group, see the suggestions given in Appendix E.

Turning Problems into Goals

PURPOSE

To enable youth
- —to look beyond their immediate reactions in a decision-making, problem-solving situation and choose among the possible alternatives
- —to use a decision-making process
- —to rethink some of the reactions they have had in decision-making situations

OUTLINE OF SESSION

Step 1—A Choice or a Reaction
Step 2—Jesus and the Syrophoenician Woman
Step 3—Solving Problems
Step 4—Prayer: Rethinking Our Reactions
(Step 5—Evaluation)

Step 1—A Choice or a Reaction

1. Tell or read the case history printed below to the group.

2. Divide the group into two groups, and assign each group one of the questions following the story.

3. Have a spokesperson for each group report on the group's thinking and answer to the question it was assigned.

Story

Darryl was sixteen years old and had quit school. He had been looking for a job for three months. A friend of his told him that he had just got a job with the A & P and that he thought that the company was still hiring. Darryl went to the local A & P where he was told to go to a downtown office. At the downtown office a receptionist gave him an application blank. When he had filled it in and given it back to her, the receptionist told him to return the next morning because the man in charge of hiring had left for the day.

Question for Group 1

Suppose that Darryl had become discouraged over the last three months and did not really believe that he would find a job. What would he think when the receptionist told him that the man in charge of hiring had left for the day? What would he do? Would he return the next morning?

Question for Group 2

Suppose that Darryl was determined to get a job. He suspected, however, that there would probably be a lot of competition for a job at the A & P. What would he be thinking when the receptionist told him to return the next morning? What would he do?

After the two groups have reported, comment:

"We can see that Darryl had a problem: he couldn't find a job. As the first group showed us, Darryl could allow himself to be overwhelmed by his problem and his feelings of discouragement and begin making decisions on the basis of what he thought might be going on around him. Or he could behave as the second group showed us and turn his problem into a goal. Let's see how we can go about turning problems into goals."

Step 2—Jesus and the Syrophoenician Woman

1. Turn to Mark 7:24-30.

2. Before beginning this step, explain:

"We are now going to look at a woman in Jesus' day who turned her problem into a goal. In order to understand this Scripture, you should know that many first-century Jews considered the Gentiles "dogs," people less worthy than themselves because the Gentiles did not follow the Jewish Law. Also, Jesus felt that he should first minister to the Jews before turning to the Gentiles."

3. Divide the group into dyads (groups of twos). Read the Bible passage and have each group of twos act it out, with one person taking the part of Jesus and the other that of the Syrophoenician woman.

4. Read the passage again, and have the actors switch roles (the person who played Jesus now plays the woman; the person who played the woman plays Jesus). Discuss the role play. Ask:

5. "How did you feel as the woman when Jesus refused your request?" (Angry, discouraged?)

6. "If you had reacted on the basis of your feeling, what would you have done?" (Left? Made an angry outburst?)

7. "As Jesus, how did you feel when the woman persisted with her request?" (That she had faith? That she would not go away until her request was granted? That she was willing to do anything to get what she wanted?)

8. "What was the problem that caused the woman to come to Jesus?" (Her daughter was sick.)

9. "What was the goal that she set for herself?" (To have Jesus heal her daughter)

10. "What did Jesus do because she persisted in her goal?" (He healed her daughter and applauded her faith.)

Comment: "The woman had a problem; her daughter was sick. She turned her problem into a goal—to have her daughter healed."

Step 3—Solving Problems

Continue: "Determining the GOAL is the first step in solving a problem or making a decision. After deciding on a goal, we can go on to look at the options, or ALTERNATIVES, open to us as solutions for the problem, what the probable CONSEQUENCES for each alternative might be—that is, what is likely to happen as a result of each alternative—and whether or not we could live with the consequences. Often, the alternative we choose in order to solve our problem depends on our VALUES, the things we think are most important. As Christians, we learn from the Bible that the most important values are those which will help us to do what is most loving. We learn that our goal in solving any problem or making a decision is to love God with all our heart, soul, and mind, and our neighbor as ourselves (Matthew 22:37, 39). Let's look at several examples to see how to go about using the problem-solving, decision-making process."

Divide the youth into two groups, and read or tell both groups one or more of the situations given below (or in Session I, Step 4). Then use the process and questions given in Session I, Step 4, for discussion.

Situation 1

Mary hung up the telephone. The minister of her church had just called. He had asked her to be one of the representatives from their denomination at a conference to be held at one of the downtown hotels. He said that there would be Christians there of all denominations all working to find solutions to some of the problems of the city. He was calling her, he said, because she always spoke up at congregational meetings and because she had once told him that she thought the churches should do something about the problems of the city.

Mary continued to stare at the telephone. Sure, she was always putting her "two cents' worth" in at the parish meeting. She knew all the people there. But she didn't know how to talk the way those big, important people do. Yet she was worried about the problems of the city. She had told the minister that she would think about it and call him back, but she still didn't know what to do. What would you do if you were Mary?

Situation 2

Don was excited. It was the Adelphi winter party. Everyone was there. Suddenly Don realized that there was at least one person present who wasn't a part of the regular crowd. There, apart from everyone else, sat Tania Reid. Who on earth would have invited her? No one was talking to her. She had just walked up to a group of people, and the entire group had moved away without speaking. Don felt sorry for her. Maybe he should go over and invite her to his table. But, then, she could be such a pest. And she hadn't the slightest idea of what to wear. Couldn't she tell that that loud sporty dress was out of place at an evening affair?

Don was undecided. If he invited her to the table, he and Shirley would be stuck with her all night long. And he wanted to have fun tonight. What should Don do?

Step 4—Prayer: Rethinking Our Reactions

Comment: "Even where our choices are limited, we can often still enjoy a certain amount of freedom and control of the outcome in a problem solving situation if we stop to choose among the alternatives. That doesn't mean that we don't feel angry or hurt or discouraged in some situations. It is normal, for example, to feel angry and discouraged if you have been looking for work for three months and are asked to come back to an employment office the next day. But it is up to you to decide what to do with your anger and discouragement. As we saw earlier, you can allow your anger and discouragement to cause you to give up, or you can become more determined to achieve your goal despite discouraging circumstances.

"For all of us there have been times when we have allowed anger or hurt or fear or pride to cause us to make an unwise decision.

1. "See yourself in the presence of Christ."
2. "Think of an instance when you allowed anger or hurt or fear or pride to cause you to make an unwise decision." (Pause)
3. "Try to feel again the way you felt at that time." (Pause)
4. "Picture that feeling; what does it look like? If you were hurt, does it look like something that has just been crushed?" (Pause)
5. "Hand the image of your feeling to Christ. Ask him to touch it and to touch you so that you are no longer overwhelmed by your feeling." (Pause)
6. "Ask him to show you how you could best have dealt with the situation." (Pause)
7. "Thank him for helping you now and for being with you and ready to help you at all times." (Pause)

Invite any who wish to discuss with the group any parts of their meditation to do so.

(Step 5—Evaluation)

To evaluate the session with members of the group, see the suggestions given in Appendix E.

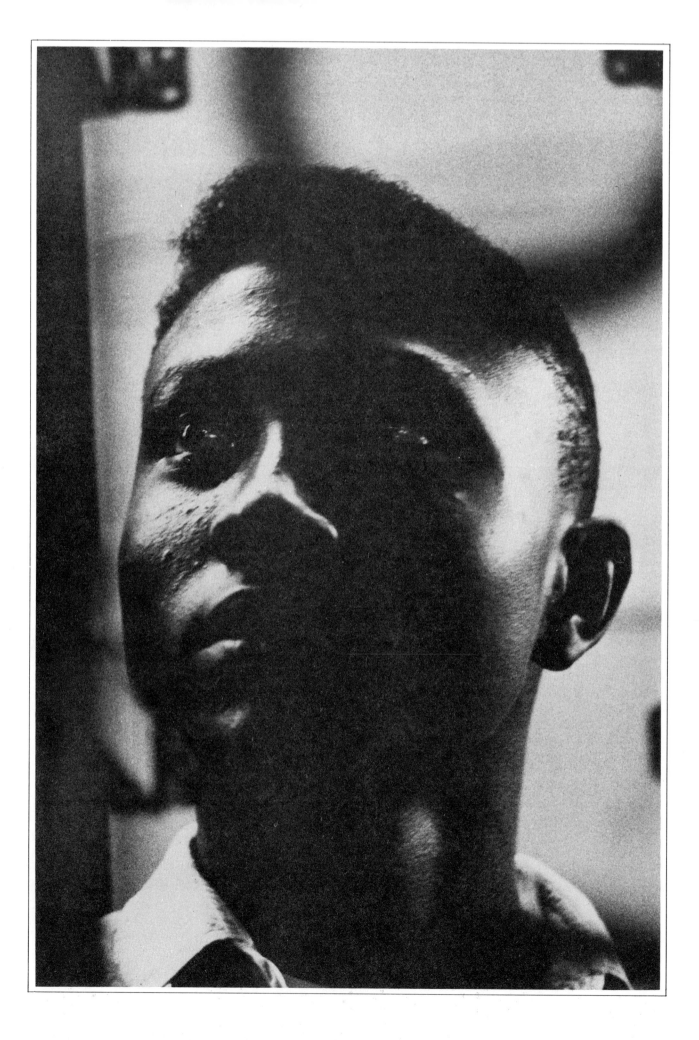

Looks Like I Won't Make It—Are You Sure?

PURPOSE

To enable youth

—to empathize with blacks in past generations who, because of discrimination, poor educational facilities, and other barriers were unable to reach their goal

—to look seriously at the goal-setting process

OUTLINE OF SESSION

Step 1—Activity: Dreams Deferred
Step 2—Can She Make It?
Step 3—Let's See
Step 4—Prayer: Lord, This Is My Goal
Step 5—Song
(Step 6—Evaluation)

Step 1—Activity: Dreams Deferred

Begin the session with this comment: "In years past many blacks were faced with barriers which made it impossible for them to reach their goals. In the South, segregation laws often forced blacks to attend poorly funded, poorly equipped schools and thus receive an inferior education, while widespread discrimination prevented them from obtaining many jobs. Thus, many blacks were unable to reach the goals which they had set for themselves. In the 1920s Langston Hughes, a black poet, wrote about the pain and frustration of some blacks who were unable to reach their goal, their dream. After you have heard some lines from his poem, try to imagine some blacks of your parents' or grandparents' or great-grandparents' generations and the goals or dreams they might have had when they were young. Then write, tell, or draw a story of a person who ended up traveling because his or her dream was deferred; or of a person who got nothing when his or her dream was deferred; or of a person whose dream was kicked around."

Read, or have someone read, the following excerpt:

I said to my baby,
Baby, take it slow.
I can't, she said, I can't!
I got to go!
  There's a certain
  amount of traveling
  in a dream deferred.
Lulu said to Leonard,
I want a diamond ring,
Leonard said to Lulu,
You won't get a goddamn thing!
  A certain

amount of nothing
in a dream deferred. . . .
From river to river
Uptown and down,
There's liable to be confusion
when a dream gets kicked around. . . .
  You talk like
  they don't kick
  dreams around
  Downtown.[1]

Discuss and share the stories and drawings.

Step 2—Can She Make It?

Opening comment: "Although conditions are much better for blacks than they were before, there are still times when we are not sure that we can reach our goals. Here is a case history of a girl who wasn't so sure."

Donna

For as long as Donna could remember, she had been interested in medicine. But it wasn't until recently, when she had had appendicitis, that she had been convinced that she wanted to be a surgeon, that she wanted to be able to stop pain and save lives by performing operations.

But Donna wasn't at all sure that she would ever get to be a surgeon. When Donna had told Dr. Adams, one of the doctors in the hospital, of her interest in surgery, he had told her much about the education and training required for surgeons and had even helped her to get an after-school job typing and filing records for a local doctor. Dr. Adams had explained that it takes about thirteen years of training after high school to become a surgeon and that had really dampened Donna's hopes. Donna's mother did day's work. Her family couldn't even afford to send her to college, much less pay for medical school. But somehow her family had scraped together all that they could, and here she was in her first year of college. Donna had hoped that she might be able to get a scholarship after her first year, and she had, in fact, taken several scholarship examinations. But she had not done well enough to win a scholarship.

Donna had made good grades in high school, but she had had to work very hard to do well in math. However, she now knew that Southern Addition, the high school she had attended, was not very good. Every year students from Southern Addition scored well

[1] From "Montage of a Dream Deferred" in *Selected Poems by Langston Hughes,* © 1951 by Langston Hughes, copyright renewed 1979. Reprinted by permission of Harold Ober Associates.

below the average on national tests, and the science department was poorly equipped. Even though Donna had made good grades in biology and chemistry, there were many things that her class had never done because the school did not have the laboratory equipment to do them. With this background Donna thought that she would be lucky if she did well enough in college to get into medical school.

Here in college she had barely been able to keep up with the math. And many other students regularly did better in science courses than she did. In the scholarship exams she had been competing against some of the class leaders as well as students from other colleges who had gone to good high schools beforehand.

Besides, she was the oldest in the family. Part of her wanted to quit school and get a job and help take some of the load off Mamma. With a good job she could help pay the rent or buy groceries. Perhaps she could even help her five younger brothers and sisters go through college. How could she ever do all those things if she were tied up in school trying to be a surgeon!

Last year, on a tour of the local hospital, Donna had had an opportunity to look at the operating room carefully and to meet and talk with an operating room technician and a nurse anesthetist. At the end of the tour the person in charge had handed out booklets which described the various health careers, what they paid, and the preparation needed for them. Now, as Donna tried to decide what to do, she turned again to the section on operating room personnel in the booklet. A general surgeon needed nine years of training after college. For the last five years, however, he or she worked in the hospital and was paid a salary. The nurse anesthetist, who gives anesthesia to the patient, must go through either the three- or the four-year training program for nurses plus a one-year hospital program created especially for nurse anesthetists.

It did not require nearly as many years to become an operating room technician, although operating room technicians must know enough about different surgical procedures to be able to make ready the right surgical instruments and equipment for the right operation. Many operating room technicians have trained for about a year to become practical nurses, have gained some experience as practical nurses, and have then taken a course for several months to become operating room technicians.

Well, there *were* other important jobs that Donna could do in the operating room besides being a surgeon. But she really wanted to be a *surgeon,* even though it didn't seem likely now that she could be. What should she do?

Step 3—Let's See

Comment: "Before we answer the question 'What should she do?' there are several things that we are going to do that might make it easier to answer the question. First, let's look at Donna's goal."

1. "What is her goal?" (To become a surgeon) "Donna seems to doubt that she can reach that goal. One way that we can decide whether it is likely that she can reach that goal is to weigh carefully the forces that would help her against those that would hinder her. That is called force-field analysis." Have a member of the group act as recorder. Have the recorder draw a line down the middle of the chalkboard or down the middle of a sheet of newsprint and write on one side "helps" and on the other "hinders."

2. "What are the things that would help Donna reach her goal?" (Her intelligence, determination, willingness and ability to work hard, her compassion, perhaps some familiarity with medical terms gained from her after-school job, etc.)

3. "What are the things that would hinder her?" (Lack of money, poor educational background, obligations to her family, etc.)

4. "Now, let's assign numerical ratings to the factors we have listed, according to the following scheme: Each factor that has almost nothing to do with attaining the goal is rated 1. Every factor that has almost nothing to do with preventing Donna from reaching the goal is also rated 1. Factors that have relatively little to do with attaining the goal or keeping Donna from the goal are rated 2. Factors that have moderate importance in attaining the goal or keeping Donna from it are rated 3. Factors rated 4 are important in attaining the goal or in keeping Donna from it. Major factors for attaining the goal or keeping Donna from it are rated 5. Have the recorder write the rating scheme on the board or on the newsprint.

5. "After each factor has been given a numerical rating, add up the points for each side, those factors which help and those which hinder. If the factors which hinder have a higher total than those which help, then it is unlikely that Donna can reach her goal." (If the factors that hinder have a higher total than those which help, continue with question 6. If not, go on to the instructions following question 9.)

6. "Are there any things that she could do to make the factors which hinder less strong?" (Get a loan; work and take night courses in things she's weak in, etc.)

7. "Now, are there any drawbacks, any negative factors in doing the things you've just suggested?" (There probably would be some drawbacks. If the participants had named the things given as examples of the answer to question 6 above, some negative factors would be that Donna would have to pay off a huge

loan, that she wouldn't be able to help her family while she was at school on a loan. Working and taking night courses would make the educational process very long.)

8. "How much, then, do you think it is possible to reduce the factors which hinder? Change the numerical ratings to show how much you think these factors can be changed."

9. "Can Donna now reach her goal?" (If members of the group feel that Donna can now reach her goal, accept that decision. Tell them, however, that the group is going to look at a procedure that Donna might use if she, in fact, decided that she could not reach her goal.)

"Let's see what would happen if she decides that it is unlikely that she can reach her goal. One of the first things a person might do if he or she realizes that the goal set is unattainable is to lower or 'scale-down' the goal. In lowering or scaling down a goal, we don't necessarily give up all that we had originally tried to obtain. But we try to obtain only a part of it for the present."

10. "How could Donna 'scale-down' her goal?" (For example, she could train to become a nurse anesthetist or an operating room technician. In these jobs Donna would still be part of a team that works in the operating room and lessens pain and saves lives. But the training for these positions requires less educational background and is shorter and thus cheaper than medical education. If the group comes up with more than one goal, have them consider each goal separately, repeating steps 11-17 below for each goal.)

11. "Let us consider each goal separately. Can Donna reach this new goal? Let's look again at the factors in the 'helps' and 'hinders' columns on the newsprint (or chalkboard)."

12. "Would the factors listed under 'helps' aid Donna in reaching this new goal?"

13. "What numerical ratings should we assign each factor? Are these the same ratings we gave them before?"

14. "Would the factors listed under 'hinders' keep Donna from reaching the new goal?

15. "What numerical ratings should we assign each factor? Are these the same ratings we gave them before?" (If the new goal[s] suggested are nurse anesthetist and operating room technician, for example, then the rating of some of the factors listed under "hinders" will change. Lack of money, for example, becomes a less important factor because the training for these jobs is shorter and thus costs less than that of a surgeon.)

16. "After each factor has been assigned a numerical rating, add up the points for each side, the 'helps' side and the 'hinders' side. If the factors which help have a higher total than those which hinder, then it is likely that Donna can reach this new goal. Can she reach it?"

17. "Does Donna have to abandon completely her original goal?" (No, she can still try to reach it. After she has earned some money as, for example, a nurse anesthetist or an operating room technician, she can pay for more education for herself as well as help support her family.)

Step 4—Prayer: Lord, This Is My Goal

"Our meditation for today can actually be an ongoing one.

"Imagine that you are in the presence of Christ.

"Think of your goal in life, your dream, what you want most." (Pause)

"Picture what your goal would look like if it is accomplished." (Pause)

"Imagine Christ in your goal picture." (Pause)

"Talk it over with him. Allow him to move into it, and change it, if that is needed." (Pause)

"Thank him for being with you always to help and lead you in everything." (Pause)

Give an opportunity for those who wish to do so to share and discuss their meditations with the group.

Step 5—Song

Sing "He's Got the Whole World in His Hands," "Lead Me, Guide Me," or some other appropriate song.

(Step 6—Evaluation)

To evaluate the session with members of the group, see the suggestions given in Appendix E.

Seeing the Whole Picture

PURPOSE

To enable youth

—to see what happens when one does not consider all the alternatives in a problem-solving, decision-making situation

—to review some personal experiences and open them to Christ to be transformed

OUTLINE OF SESSION

Step 1—Simulation Game: "Left Back"
Step 2—Discussion: Being Left Back
Step 3—"Stand Fast in Freedom"
Step 4—"Christ Has Made You Free" (Prayer)
Step 5—Song
(Step 6—Evaluation)

In this session members of the group will play a simulation game, "Left Back." Materials for this game are found in Appendix C. Some preparations must be made before the game can be played. The game board, spinner, tokens, and cards for two teams and for the judge are included in the Appendix. It would probably be best to paste the page including the game board and the half page including the spinner and tokens on a piece of cardboard and then cut them out so that they will be easier to use. This can also be done with the game cards. If you do paste the game card pages on cardboard before cutting them out, the number of the card will have to be written in on the cardboard backing. Mark each card clearly on the back with the appropriate color—red, green, or blue—for easy identification. A pin or thumbtack can be placed through the middles of the arrow and spinner cards to make the spinner workable. Have these things ready when the session begins. Be sure that none of the players sees the cards before the game is played.

In this game the players are asked as members of a team to make choices dealing with some major decision-making areas in life. The object of the game is to see which team can reach the goal, labeled "A Fulfilling Life," first. Unknown to the players, the members of the team with the red cards have only a limited number of alternatives for making their decisions, and none of the options which those on this team have adequately solves the problem facing them. The green-card team has been given a larger number of options. Some of the alternatives on their cards provide good solutions to the problem they are asked to solve. Each answer allows the team to move forward one or more spaces, remain where they are, or move

backward. The judge's cards, which are blue, list all the solutions given to both teams along with the moves awarded each answer. Play continues until one team has reached the goal. Of course, the team with the larger number of options "wins" the game. It is hoped that the players will learn from this experience that a wide range of options is important for making decisions and that people who do not consider a wide range of options or alternatives, for whatever reason, often make decisions or choose solutions which do not adequately solve the problems they face.

Step 1—Simulation Game: "Left Back"

1. Choose one person as judge for the game. The judge is given the set of blue cards listing the moves awarded for the answers which the teams will give when their tokens land on decision-making blocks.

2. Divide the remaining participants into two teams.

3. Explain that in this game each team will be asked to make choices dealing with some major decision-making areas in life. Each team has a turn to spin the spinner to determine how many squares the team's token may be moved forward. Whenever its token lands on a numbered square on the game board, a team selects from its set of cards the one card that has the same number as that square. From the list of options printed on the card, the team as a group selects a single option. It may not choose an option that isn't listed on the card. When the team announces its choice, the judge, who has a blue card with the same number on it, reads from that card what move the team may make with the option selected. The team will then move its token forward, remain in the same square, or move backward, according to the instructions given by the judge. The object of the game is to see which team can reach the goal, labeled "A Fulfilling Life," first.

4. Have each team spin the spinner to determine who goes first. High number takes the red cards and goes first. The team spinning the lower number takes the green cards.

5. Have each team pick up its token and put it on the square marked "Go." Begin play. Note: If at any time a team token lands on a numbered, decision-making square for which that team has already made a choice, then a team member simply spins the spinner again and moves the token ahead according to the second spin.

6. After the participants have played the game once, expose all the choice cards to everyone and have the

group discuss these questions:

a. What happened in the game?

b. Why did the green team win the game?

7. Tell the youth: "We are going to play the game over again, but this time those who were the green team will be the red team, and those who were the red team will be the green team." Encourage the red team to try to win against "the system," and remind its members that they can only give the answers printed on their choice cards.

Step 2—Discussion: Being Left Back

After the second play is finished, have the youth use the following questions for discussion:

1. "Now both teams have had the chance to be both the team with the advantage and the deprived team. How did you feel when you were on the red team? About yourself? About the other team? About the game? About the other people on your team?"

2. "How did you feel knowing that you were being cheated?"

3. "When you were on the green team, how did you feel? About yourself? About the other team? About the game? About the other people on your team?"

4. "If the game had been real life and you had been on the red team, do you think the feelings you were experiencing would have been helpful or harmful as you tried to deal with the life situations? Why?"

5. "If you had been on the green team, do you think the feelings you were experiencing would have been helpful or harmful? Why?"

6. "What did you learn from the game and from this discussion?"

7. Give a summary of the following:

The game itself, of course, tells us something about a real-life situation which many black people face. There are many black people who do not have a wide range of options open to them when they make decisions which affect their lives. Because many blacks live in communities where schooling is poor, some are not even aware of many excellent possibilities when they make their decisions. Because most blacks have less resources—less money, less influence, etc.—than many whites do, some options are not open to them. Most important, until relatively recently, many blacks have been legally deprived of the opportunity to make decisions for themselves. Both slavery and legal segregation, along with widespread discrimination, imposed severe limitations on black decision making. Because they have become used to having other people make their decisions for them, some blacks simply don't bother to look at the options and make decisions for themselves. They allow circumstances to make the decision for them. If, however, they are willing to investigate as many of the possible options as they can, they will find that they have a better opportunity to control or influence the decisions which affect their lives.

Step 3—"Stand Fast in Freedom"

Have the youth first read, or have someone read aloud, Genesis 2:15-17; 3:1-6, 9-19; and Romans 5:12-14.

1. "What kind of decision did Adam and Eve make? Was it a good decision or a bad one? According to the Genesis account and the verses from Romans, what was the result of that decision for Adam and Eve and for the rest of the human race?"

Now, have the group read Deuteronomy 5:12-14; Mark 3:1-6; and Luke 13:10-17.

2. "According to these passages, how does it seem the Pharisees and lawyers went about making decisions?"

3. "How do you think Jesus went about making the decisions he made?"

4. "Which method do you think was freer, less constrained? Paul in Galatians 5:1 tells us as Christians to 'stand fast therefore in the liberty wherewith Christ hath made us free.' Now, suppose in the game we just played both the red and the green teams had had exactly the same option cards, but the members of the green team had refused at each decision-making point to consider any of the options except the last two listed on the card. Which of the teams seems to you to be approaching decision making with an attitude similar to the one Paul suggests to the Galatians?"

5. "If the green team insisted on making decisions by considering only the last two options on the card, who would have limited the green team's freedom?"

6. "What does this teach us concerning our real-life decision making as Christians?" (That we must not limit our own freedom in decision making by considering only a small number of the possible alternatives.)

Step 4—"Christ Has Made You Free" (Prayer)

1. Have the members of the group imagine that they are in the presence of Christ. (Pause)

2. Ask them to recall a situation in the past where they have made a decision without considering carefully all of the options open to them. (Pause)

3. Have them reexplore the situation with Christ. What were the options? Which would have been the best choice? (Pause)

4. Ask them to ask Christ to help them choose whenever they have a decision to make. (Pause) Allow those who wish to share and discuss their meditation with the group to do so.

Step 5—Song

Sing "Free at Last" or some other appropriate song.

(Step 6—Evaluation)

To evaluate the session with members of the group, see the suggestions given in Appendix E.

A Long-Term Project: Decision Making for Teens and Preteens

God's Revelation: "Choose this day. . . ." (Joshua
    24:15).

Our Response: Where am I faced with choices, and
    how do I go about choosing?

At least five meetings are needed to carry out this
long-term project, plus additional time set aside for the
religious celebration. If all the outlined sessions for the
unit are used and a mid-project revision scheduled, the
long-term project will require at least nine meetings in
addition to the time set aside for the religious
celebration. The nine-meeting outline is given below.
Any of the outlined sessions can, of course, be omitted.

SAMPLE OUTLINE

Meeting 1—Commitment Service (see Appendix F)
        and Session IV

Meeting 2—Session I

Meeting 3—Session II

Meeting 4—Session III

Meeting 5—Plan the social action project

Meeting 6—Discuss ways to cope with negative
        aspects of the social action project; plan
        home devotions

Meeting 7—Plan and prepare for a religious
        celebration on the theme
        —Celebration

Meeting 8—Mid-project revision

Meeting 9—Evaluation

SOCIAL ACTION PROJECT SUGGESTIONS

There are many areas where youth are called on to
make decisions. Some of these include such areas as
career and vocation, the church (in the life of the
congregation and in the life of the denomination or
larger church body), and social life (e.g., dress, dating,
sex). After the members of the group have researched
the decisions to be made in these areas, they could
present a program, put together a newssheet, or in
some other way make available the information
concerning options and consequences for the benefit of
other youth in the community.

SOME SUGGESTIONS FOR RESEARCHING THE PROJECTS

For whatever area they choose, the youth can adapt
the decision-making, problem-solving process outlined in Sessions I and II, or some other decision
making process, to help them in their task. In some
areas (for example, for decisions to be made in the life

of the church), the youth may have to determine what
kinds of decisions they will be called on to make before
they can actually begin using the decision-making
process.

Decision Making About Career and Vocation

Decisions in the area of career and vocation often
involve decisions concerning education and training.

Libraries, high school counselors, and job counselors at employment agencies all offer information
concerning various careers, what is involved in them,
what training or type of education is required, what opportunities are available in the field, etc.

Decision Making in the Life of the Church

Decision making in the life of the church may
involve questions in many areas of concern. Some of
these include faith and doctrine (for example, "What is
the teaching of the church in this current question?"),
worship ("What time shall we hold services? How
should we go about adapting our liturgy to reflect
current thought and speech patterns?"), mission
("What is the mission of the people of God assembled
in this place?"), program ("How do we go about
carrying out this mission? Which components of it are
most important and which are least important?"),
budget ("What material resources do we need to carry
out our mission? What can we reasonably expect?
Which parts of the program, if any, must we curtail or
eliminate?").

Many denominational headquarters have available
printed information concerning the working of the
church and decision making in the church. One such
booklet is called "A Study Guide" and concerns youth
participation in conventions and other church bodies.
It is available from the Staff Officer for Youth
Ministries, The Episcopal Church Center, 815 Second
Avenue, New York, NY 10017. You may also want to
contact the clergy and members of the congregational
governing board (vestry, board of trustees, board of
deacons, etc.) to explain some of the local decision-
making processes to the youth and perhaps to train
them to participate in the board as youth representatives.

Decision Making About Social Life (dress, dating, sex, etc.)

- Conduct a survey or assemble a panel composed
  of parents, youth, local school officials, doctors,
  ministers, etc., to explore and give opinions on the

various options and alternatives in these areas.

- Ask each member of the group to dialogue with his or her parents, or have a group discussion among the youth and parents concerning their opinions of the various options and alternatives open in these areas.

COPING WITH NEGATIVE ASPECTS

Even after a seemingly careful and painstaking consideration of options and alternatives and consequences, some members of the group may still make choices which do not seem warranted from an objective evaluation of all the information available. A discussion with the whole group of all the decisions made, the options open, and the feelings involved in making the decisions may, perhaps, be helpful. See also Appendix H, "Coping with Negative Aspects in a Social Action Project," for additional suggestions.

HOME DEVOTIONS

In addition to the biblical passages and meditations given in the outlined sessions, the following Bible passages may be useful for home devotions: Deuteronomy 30:11-20; Psalm 119:30; Proverbs 3:31; 16:16; and 22:1; and Luke 10:38-42. Prayers from *The Book of Common Prayer* which are appropriate for this theme include Propers 5 (p. 229), 10 (p. 231), 14 (p. 232), and 19 (p. 233), and the prayers for guidance (57 and 58, p. 832). For additional suggestions concerning home devotions, see Appendix I.

CELEBRATION

At the institution of the Lord's Supper, Christ with thanksgiving made an offering of his own life to make possible a new life of love, freedom, justice, peace, and joy for all human beings. Every celebration of Eucharist, or Holy Communion, presents Christians with the decision as to whether or not they, as members of the church—the Body of Christ, with Christ the Head—will offer what God has given them—time, talent, and money—back to God for the work of bringing new life. Of course, this is a decision which is presented to every Christian many times each day. But the Christian makes this decision publicly, formally, and intentionally when he or she offers with Christ what God has given him or her and receives, in receiving Christ, the grace and strength to carry on his work in the world. At the special service for this unit, members of the youth group can show publicly, formally, and intentionally that the decisions they are undertaking will, in fact, involve an offering of what God has given them for the continuing work of Christ in the world. For general comments on using the Eucharist, or Holy Communion, for the celebration, see Appendix J.

MUSIC

In addition to the hymns suggested in the outlined sessions, these hymns are also appropriate for the theme: "I've Decided to Make Jesus My Choice," "Where He Leads Me," "Done Made My Vow to the Lord."

EVALUATION

See "Suggestions for Project Evaluation," Appendix L.

Unit on Faith

Background

2

Faith has been the basis of life for black people in America for the last three hundred years. For black Americans, faith has seldom been simply an intellectual assent to a body of principles or beliefs. Rather, faith for blacks has been more often characterized by a deep trust in God which allows the person to risk in order to do what he or she believes to be God's will. Session I in this unit explores the nature of faith, this deep trust in God and willingness to risk, as seen both in biblical personages and in the lives of blacks both past and present. In Session II we see faith as an element which can also be used by the faithful to help sustain others and enable them to reach their goals.

Faith, as seen in the lives of Frederick Douglass and Harriet Tubman, cited in Sessions I and II, has resulted in dramatic action. But based on a belief in a God who wills that all people should live in a world where justice, peace, love, freedom, and total well-being prevail, and in the certainty that God can work to bring into being this desired world, the faith of the Afro-American has been expressed not only in dramatic action but in heroic endurance as well. Countless thousands of blacks have waited patiently on the Lord as, shackled by injustice and discrimination, they have been willing to meet and face frustration every day, confident that the One who has provided in the past will provide for them in the future also. That kind of faith involves a willingness to risk. It involves a willingness to risk cynicism, despair, and madness as one reaffirms the vision of a world that seems destined never to come.

In this unit the long-term projects provide an opportunity for members of the youth group to reach out into the community, to act in faith, and to mirror God's faithfulness.

For, ultimately, as is shown in Session III, it is God who is the Faithful One. Whatever faith we have comes from God and is only a faint reflection of God's eternal faithfulness. It is God whom we can trust to be with us always. It is God who trusts us enough to risk giving us the freedom to make our own decisions. When those decisions lead us away, God forgives us and welcomes us back again to a life of trust, freedom, and love. Through faith in God and faith from God, we as black people can continue the struggle for freedom in America and the right to influence the decisions which will enable us to live creative and meaningful lives here.

Now, as we see our people and others who are poor and unable to make any impact upon decisions which affect our lives—decisions which, for example, abolish jobs in order to keep profits high—we realize that we must continue to act in faith not only for our own benefit but to sustain others as well.

Trust—and Willingness to Risk

PURPOSE

To enable youth to explore the nature of faith as trust and risk

OUTLINE OF SESSION

Step 1—Is This the Road?
Step 2—Abraham
Step 3—Black Mystery Guest OR Jennie Mae
Step 4—Litany: "So Great a Cloud of Witnesses"
Step 5—Song
Step 6—Activity: Collage
(Step 7—Evaluation)

Step 1—Is This the Road?

1. Divide the entire group into groups of twos.
2. Give the following background for the game:

"This is a game which is played in West Africa when two children are coming home from an errand, have gone visiting, or for some other reason have left home.

"One person closes his or her eyes and is led by the other one. The leader is careful to see that the one with eyes closed doesn't run into anything or trip and fall. Along the way the one with eyes closed stops to touch trees or other objects and asks, 'Have we reached home?' The one who is leading answers, 'No, it's the road.' When the one with eyes closed thinks that he or she has finally reached home, he or she asks, 'Have we reached home or haven't we?' The leader will answer, 'We have gotten there' when they have reached home only if the person with eyes closed has asked the question, 'Have we reached home or haven't we?'"

3. In each group of two have one person be the leader and the other the one who is led with eyes closed. Before starting, while all eyes are still open, arrange chairs and tables for "trees" to touch along the way, and have everyone determine where "home" is. Then begin the game. As couples finish, have them watch those who are still playing.

4. Lead a discussion with these questions. To those who had their eyes closed: "Could you tell where you were going?" (No, not if their eyes were really closed.)

"How did you know that you would ever reach 'home?'" (Had to trust the one who was leading.)

"In walking around with your eyes closed, you risked falling over tables and chairs. Weren't you afraid that you would fall?" (No, because I knew that the person who was leading me would see to it that I didn't fall.)

Step 2—Abraham

Having faith is a lot like being the one with eyes closed in the game "Is This the Road?" Often, although we cannot see just exactly what is going to happen in the future, we are able to take the risks which God requires of us. We can take these risks just as we did in the game because we trust God to care for us and to see that we don't fall.

"In the Old Testament Abraham was a man of faith, one who was able to take the risks God required of him because he trusted God. Abraham was a man who believed that God wanted him to do something special. He believed that God wanted him to leave his homeland and go to a new land where his people would live for centuries to come.

"Abraham could not be certain that he would find a land where his people could settle. But because he trusted God, he and his family set out and God eventually brought them to Canaan, the Promised Land. God promised that Abraham would be given many descendants, but Abraham's wife, Sarah, had no children. Finally, when they were very old, Sarah had a son, Isaac.

"In the new land to which God had led Abraham, many people sacrificed their children to the gods they worshiped. Abraham thought that he, too, should sacrifice his only son, Isaac, to his God. But as Abraham was about to kill Isaac, he discovered that God did not want this sacrifice. He discovered that his God, our God, does not demand such unreasonable and inhumane service. Abraham was willing to risk the possibility that he would not find a new land to settle, and he was willing to risk his son Isaac's life because he trusted God."

Step 3—(Alternative A) Black Mystery Guest

1. Put seventeen pieces of newsprint on the wall, leaving a space between the ninth and tenth pieces of paper. Or draw seventeen large blocks on the chalkboard, leaving a space between the ninth and tenth blocks. (The paper or blocks are for the letters in the name of the mystery guest, Frederick Douglass. The letters will fit into the blocks in this way: (1) F, (2) r, (3) e, (4) d, (5) e, (6) r, (7) i, (8) c, (9) k, space, (10) D, (11) o, (12) u, (13) g, (14) l, (15) a, (16) s, (17) s. However, DO NOT put the letters in the blocks at this time.)
2. Divide the group into two groups.
3. Introduce the game:

"Throughout our history in this country, there have been many great black men and women of faith. In this game you will have a chance to guess the identity of one of these people. By turns, first one group and then the other will suggest a letter of the alphabet which may be in this person's name. If your guess is correct, I will print the letter in the block where it belongs in the name and give you a clue to the person's identity and an opportunity to guess who it is. If your group suggests a letter that is not in the name or, after the clue is given, doesn't guess the person's identity correctly, the turn goes to the other group. Before suggesting a letter and before trying to guess the person's name, group members should decide together what answer they will give."

4. Begin the game.
The clues:
• born a slave in Maryland
• persuaded white school boys to teach him to read
• talked with a religious old black man who told him to pray for freedom since God had a great work for him to do
• despite the dangers posed by slave catchers and trained bloodhounds, decided to escape from slavery
• sent to jail when another slave told of his escape plans
• was released from jail and made a successful escape from slavery
• became a lay minister
• became an abolitionist in the North, speaking at antislavery meetings
• became editor of an antislavery newspaper
• spoke in Europe against slavery
• as an adviser to President Lincoln, persuaded the president to allow blacks to fight in the Union Army during the Civil War
• after the war went to Haiti as representative of the U.S.

5. If the mystery guest's identity is guessed before all the clues are given, either ask the team giving the correct identity to tell the group the rest of Frederick Douglass's life or read the rest of the clues for the benefit of those who don't know Douglass's story.

Step 3—(Alternative B) Jennie Mae

Read or tell the group the following case history.

Jennie Mae was a high school student who had gone one day during the summer vacation to clean for Mrs. Jones. Mrs. Jones taught at Centerville High School and normally employed Jennie Mae's mother to clean for her on Thursdays. However, Jennie Mae's mother was sick and had sent Jennie Mae in her stead. At lunchtime Mrs. Jones began to talk to the girl about her plans for the future. Jennie Mae told the teacher that she wanted to become a hospital dietitian. Mrs. Jones asked Jennie Mae what grades she had received in school so far. Jennie Mae told her that she had very good grades in math and science, but that she had not done well in English. She explained that she wasn't interested in English and had stopped writing reports for English classes because the teachers had frequently harshly criticized the reports from black students in front of the class. Mrs. Jones replied that she didn't think that Jennie Mae should try to go to college. It was expensive; and since there was a lot of writing to do in college, she might flunk out. "Besides," she added, "you'll just have to come back to cook in someone's kitchen, even if you do get all that training. Centerville Hospital doesn't have any Negro dietitians."

Jennie Mae became more and more concerned. Although Mrs. Jones had prepared a lot of students for college and knew a lot about what was expected in courses there, Jennie Mae suspected that Mrs. Jones had advised her not to try to go to college largely because she was black. Of course, college was expensive. Perhaps she shouldn't take all that money away from the family, when she might fail anyway. What would you do?

In addition to discussing what Jennie Mae should do, have the group discuss the following:

1. "How do you think Jennie Mae felt after she had talked to Mrs. Jones?" (Frightened, discouraged about her future, angry with Mrs. Jones?)

2. "How do you think Jennie Mae's feelings might affect her faith in herself and in what she might be able to do in the future?" (She might lose her faith in herself, be unwilling to take risks in the future.)

3. "What are some of the things that we can do at times like this when we lose our faith in ourselves?" (Pray; talk with parents, teachers, ministers, and others whose faith is strong and who have the skills to help us; read the lives of men and women who have reached their goals despite many obstacles.)

Step 4—Litany: "So Great a Cloud of Witnesses"

With the members of the group giving the responses, recite the following litany:

O God, Creator, Redeemer, Sanctifier,
Have mercy on us.
For your love and continuing presence among us,
We thank you, O Lord.
For the many men and women who have been willing to risk because they trusted in you,
We thank you, O Lord.
For Abraham and Frederick Douglass and other men and women throughout the ages whose faith has been strong,

We thank you, O Lord.
For parents and teachers and friends who believe in us and are willing to help and support us when our faith grows weak,
We thank you, O Lord.
That we may be willing to risk and dare in your name,
We pray to you, Lord God.
That we may always be mindful of your loving presence and care,
We pray to you, Lord God.
Let us commend ourselves and one another to God.
To you, O Lord our God. Amen.

Step 5—Song

Sing "We've Come This Far by Faith," "I Will Trust in the Lord," "He's Got the Whole World in His Hands," or another appropriate song.

Step 6—Activity: Collage

1. Have available magazines, colored construction paper, pencils and pens, scissors, and paste.

2. Have each member of the group choose, cut out, draw, or otherwise make one set of shapes and colors which seem to him or her to go with willingness to risk and another set which goes with trust.

3. Have each person make a collage with the shapes and colors designating trust surrounding those standing for willingness to risk.

4. With masking tape mount the collages around the room.

5. Have each person discuss his or her collage and why he or she decided to use the shapes or colors chosen.

6. Ask each person to take home his or her collage and to use it as a reminder of faith when a faith crisis comes about.

(Step 7—Evaluation)

To evaluate the session with members of the group, see the suggestions given in Appendix E.

Session II

Faith for Others

PURPOSE

To enable youth
—to see how the faith of one person at times helps others to reach their goals
—to explore the nature of trust

OUTLINE OF SESSION

Step 1—Harriet Tubman
Step 2—Discussion
Step 3—Whom Do You Trust?
Step 4—"When He Saw Their Faith . . ."
Step 5—Activity: Costumes and Scenery
(Step 6—Evaluation)

This session serves as the preparation for an actual production of a drama based on the life of Harriet Tubman. In presenting this drama, the group can bring to the attention of the congregation, their parents, and friends the faithful witness of courageous and spirit-filled blacks in the past.

Since the presentation is a creative drama, there are no lines to be learned. The members of the group simply listen to the story of Harriet Tubman, decide on the scenes necessary for portraying the story, and make up or create appropriate dialogue and action for the scenes. However, the group will have to make scenery and costumes if the drama is to be performed before an audience. Have available for the session old clothing and cloth which can easily be made into costumes; furniture which would be appropriate for the suggested scenes; a stapler, paper, cardboard, paints, and crayons for creating trees and other natural scenery and for making posters to advertise the production; and any other materials which would be useful in making scenery and costumes.

Step 1—Harriet Tubman

1. Read or tell the group the following story of Harriet Tubman's life.

2. Have the group decide which scenes would best portray this story in a drama (see suggestions below).

3. Decide which characters are necessary to portray the story, and choose persons to play the characters. Be sure to choose a narrator, also, who can fill in for the audience important details which will not be shown in the scenes.

4. Have the players walk through the scenes, creating dialogue and actions which they feel will tell the story.

Harriet Tubman

Harriet Tubman was born a slave. When she was still a small child, her master, in a fit of anger, threw a heavy weight at her, hitting her in the head. Her mother nursed her until she was well, but from that time on, Harriet was subject to sleeping spells. Whenever she sat down, she was likely to fall asleep. From her mother, though, Harriet learned a practice which she would continue for the rest of her life: she learned to pray continually and to ask God's blessing on whatever she was doing.

While she was still a girl, Harriet's master hired her out to work for other whites. Once, when she was hired out as a baby nurse, she was whipped three times because she could not clean a room to the satisfaction of the woman who had hired her. Finally, the woman's sister showed Harriet how to clean. However, Harriet was soon returned to her master as worthless: Every time she sat down to rock the baby, she fell asleep!

After Harriet's master died, a rumor circulated among the slaves that Harriet and her two brothers were to be sold in the Deep South. The three decided to run away. Each of them slipped away to a meeting place in the woods to begin the journey together. However, as they went on, Harriet's brothers began to think of the horrible punishment which they would receive if they were caught, and one after the other, Harriet's brothers turned back. Hiding during the day and using the North Star to guide her at night, Harriet went on alone to Philadelphia.

Although she found work in Philadelphia, Harriet was still not satisfied. She wanted other slaves to live in freedom as she did. Nineteen times Harriet slipped back to the South to rescue more than 300 other black people from slavery. Hidden in slave cabins, she talked with such excitement of the life of freedom that even women with babies were willing to follow her to the North. Many of the slaves became frightened along the way, but Harriet insisted that they continue. She even threatened to shoot those who wanted to be left along the way to prevent them from telling anyone the routes she took. She assured her followers that they were quite safe since she only went where Jesus led her. Harriet was even able to bring her aged parents out of slavery in a horse-drawn, two-wheeled cart. Finally, the slave owners in the Maryland district from which she stole so many slaves offered a $40,000 reward for her capture, dead or alive.

Harriet purchased a small home in Auburn, New

York, where she cared for her parents and other homeless, elderly people who were brought to her. However, during the Civil War, Governor Andrew of Massachusetts asked her to go south again to act as a spy and scout for the Union Army. She also served as a nurse for men wounded in battle. Every night, though, Harriet made pies and gingerbread and root beer and sold them to the troops so that she could support the elderly people at her home in New York. And, after the war, she had a friend publish the story of her life so that she could pay the mortgage on her home and thus assure that her old people could continue to live there.

When, as a very old woman, Harriet Tubman died, the people of Auburn, New York, erected a monument to her. On the monument they wrote that "with implicit trust in God, she braved every danger and overcame every obstacle."

Some Suggested Scenes

- Harriet hired out as a baby nurse
- Harriet and her brothers running away
- Harriet encouraging other slaves to escape and leading them to freedom
- Harriet with the Union Army during the Civil War
- Harriet with her old people

Step 2—Discussion

After the group has acted out the drama, lead a discussion of the faith element in Harriet Tubman's life, using these questions:

1. Why did Harriet Tubman risk her life time and time again to help slaves escape? What made it possible for her to do that?

2. What do you think frightened slaves were thinking as Harriet led them to freedom?

3. Do you think Harriet was ever frightened? Is it possible to have faith and yet be frightened?

4. Do you think that you would have been willing to trust Harriet Tubman to bring you safely to the North? If so, why? If not, why?

Step 3—Whom Do You Trust?

1. Give each member of the group a piece of paper and a pencil.

2. Comment that in this step the group is going to explore what it is that makes us willing to trust another person.

3. Ask each person to write on the paper the name of the person whom he or she trusts most ("my mother," "my friend," etc.) and the reason why he or she trusts that person.

4. Place the sheets of paper in the middle of the group. Ask one person to read the answers as another

person records them on newsprint or on the chalkboard.

5. Note which persons the members of the group seem to trust most (parents, friends, teachers, etc.) and which qualities in these persons tend to make them worthy of trust.

Step 4—"When He Saw Their Faith . . ."

1. Comment that it is often our faith in others and in *their* faith in God which helps us to reach our goals.

2. Turn to Luke 5:17-26. Ask the members of the group to pretend that they are one of the men, in the passage to be read, who is bringing the sick person to Jesus. Have the group members try to imagine how they would feel as they carry the man on his litter to Jesus.

3. Read the passage slowly. Then ask the members of the group to describe how they felt as they brought the man to Christ. Did he get heavy on the way? Did they feel that it was too much trouble to take the roof apart to let him down to Jesus? Did they feel at any point that they wanted to give up? How did they feel when they realized that it was their faith to which Jesus responded in curing the man?

4. Have the members of the group imagine that they are in the presence of Christ. (Pause)

5. Have them think of the people in their lives (family, friends, others) who might be depending on their faith to reach the goals which they have set. (Pause)

6. Ask the members of the group to recall the qualities which they must have in order that others will trust them. (Pause) Have them think of the qualities they will need, also, if their faith is going to enable another to reach his or her goal. (Pause)

7. Have them ask Christ to give them the qualities which are necessary if they are to have the faith to sustain others. (Pause)

Step 5—Activity: Costumes and Scenery

1. Have the group make the costumes and scenery necessary for an actual production of the Harriet Tubman drama.

2. Have someone write a narrator's part which will give continuity to the different scenes and present important details which are not included in the scenes. You may also wish to include in the narrator's part some of the insights concerning a faith for others, which were brought out in Steps 2, 3, and 4 above.

3. If a date for the presentation of the drama has been agreed upon, have some of the youth make posters to advertise the production.

4. Practice the play again, or set a date when the group can come together to practice.

(Step 6—Evaluation)

To evaluate the session with the members of the group, see the suggestions given in Appendix E.

Imaging God

PURPOSE

To enable youth
—to see God as One who trusts and can be trusted
—to see themselves in the image of God

OUTLINE OF SESSION

Step 1—Making Puppets
Step 2—"The Tricky Tortoise"
Step 3—God Trusts: The Prodigal Son
Step 4—And We Can Trust God: The Twenty-Third Psalm
Step 5—Prayer: In the Image of God, One Who Trusts and Can Be Trusted
(Step 6—Evaluation)

In this session the group will make sock puppets for a puppet show. Bring to the session enough old socks for all the puppets needed, some buttons, tape, yarn, glue, pieces of fabric, paper, pipe cleaners, Magic Markers, small bells, and needles and thread. (You may wish to make a separate puppet for each of the many-headed Babalawos mentioned in the story. You can use one puppet and attach with tape an additional head—a pipe cleaner with a paper face on it—before each entrance of the Babalawo.) Have available also a large table which can serve as the puppet stage and small cardboard boxes which can be made into market stalls for scenery.

Step 1—Making Puppets

1. Read the story "The Tricky Tortoise" to the group (see below).
2. Assign some members of the group to make the puppets to be used in the puppet show in Step 2 (the tortoise, with small bells or noisemakers covering him; several market women; one or more Babalawos with attachable heads. It is not necessary to try to dress the puppets in Yoruba costume).
3. Have several members of the group make scenery. Small cardboard boxes with paper representations of fruit, vegetables, or cloth taped on can serve as market stalls.

Step 2—"The Tricky Tortoise"

"The Tricky Tortoise" is a cantefable, a tale with a song, which is told by the Yoruba of Nigeria. The ancestors of the present-day black Americans came from West Africa, and some may even have been Yoruba.

Although today many Yoruba are Christians, traditionally they believed in many gods. One of these gods was the god of fate, or of chance. The Yoruba went to the Babalawo, the priest of the god of fate, to find out what they should do in any situation.

The markets in Nigeria are not like our supermarkets. They are open-air and are often very, very large. Most of the sellers in Nigeria are women. They either rent or buy a space in the marketplace where they make stalls out of wooden tables and crates. There they exhibit fruits, vegetables, cooking oils, meat, cotton goods, or whatever they have to sell. This is a story about the tortoise who goes to market. Many tales are told about Tortoise among the Yoruba. He is a favorite trickster character.

The Tricky Tortoise

One day, Tortoise heard of a market which was only for women. Tortoise decided that he would attend the market even though men were not supposed to go. He knew that lepers always wear noisemakers to warn people to stay away from them. Tortoise decided to dress up with noisemakers all over his body.

When he arrived at the market, he began to sing the song (at the bottom of the next page) in a false voice.

All the women who buy and sell in the market were frightened away by the noisemakers and the singing, and while they were gone, Tortoise ate up all the food they were selling. Tortoise was careful to leave before the market women came back, but he returned the next day and for many days after that.

The market women got poorer and poorer because Tortoise was eating up all their wares. Finally, they went to the Babalawo and told him what was happening. The Babalawo came to the market the next day to fight with the tortoise, but in the fight, Tortoise killed him. Two, three, four, five, six, seven, eight, and nine-headed Babalawos fought Tortoise but were all killed by him. The ten-headed Babalawo, however, pulled Tortoise's disguise off him. When the market women, who were watching the fight, saw that the great thief was only a tortoise, they began to beat him with a stick. It is because of this beating that the tortoise has a broken-looking shell even to this day.

1. Have the group set up the scenery on a large table which will serve as the puppet stage.
2. Choose people to play the various characters in the tale.
3. Practice the song with the person who will play Tortoise.

4. Have the players kneel on the floor behind the table and act out the tale, making up the dialogue as they go along. If you wish, you can hang a thin curtain behind the table so that the players' heads are hidden from view, but the players are able to see what is happening on the stage. If the group wishes to present the play for an audience, it can practice again after the session.

Step 3—God Trusts: The Prodigal Son

Summarize these comments:

"In 'The Tricky Tortoise' we were able to learn something about the life of the ancestors of black Americans who lived in West Africa. We were also able to learn something about puppets. We made the puppets and put them on the stage. When we moved our hands a certain way, the puppet moved that way. When we spoke, the puppet spoke.

"God made us and brought us into the world which God had made. But God does not treat us as puppets. One of the places where Jesus shows us how God relates to human beings is in the story of the prodigal son."

1. Divide the youth into three groups. One group represents the father in the story and will answer all questions addressed to him. The second group represents the younger son and the third group the older son.

2. Turn to Luke 15:11-32.

3. Read verses 11-13a. Ask the group representing the father to describe how they think the father felt in this situation.

4. Read verses 13b-16. Ask the group representing the younger son how he felt at this point.

5. Read verses 17-24. Ask the group representing the younger son how they think the younger son felt about his father at this point.

6. Read verses 25-27. Ask the third group representing the older son how he felt.

7. Read verses 28-32. Ask all the groups: Do you think the father cheated the older son? What does the story show us about how God relates to human beings?

Be sure to point out, if it is not mentioned, that the story shows that God trusts us to make our own decisions and forgives and welcomes us back when these decisions lead us away from God.

Step 4—And We Can Trust God: The Twenty-Third Psalm

Opening comment: "We have seen that God trusts

[1] Teremuje: a nonsense word pronounced "Tare-ray-moo-jay."

35

us. Now we shall see that we can trust God, too."

Have the group turn to Psalm 23 and list all the reasons given there which show why we can trust God (God keeps us from want, leads us to do what is right, etc.).

Step 5—Prayer: In the Image of God, One Who Trusts and Can Be Trusted

1. Remind the group that we are made in the image of God and that just as God trusts us and can be trusted, we are expected to mirror the image of God on earth and develop with others relationships in which we can trust and be trusted.

2. Have the youth picture themselves in the presence of Christ. (Pause)

3. Have them think of one person with whom they would like to develop a relationship in which they can trust and be trusted. (Pause)

4. Have the group recall the qualities which make God One whom we can trust. (Pause)

5. Have them ask Christ to show them how to develop these qualities. (Pause)

6. Have the group recall what it is that shows us that God trusts us. (Pause)

7. Have them ask Christ to help them to develop the ability to trust as God trusts us. (Pause)

(Step 6—Evaluation)

To evaluate the session with the group, see the suggestions given in Appendix E.

A Long-Term Project: Doing Something in Faith

God's Revelation: "... be thou faithful unto death ..." (Revelation 2:10).

Our Response: What is faith? How can we best act in faith and mirror God's faithfulness to others?

A long-term project in this unit can cover at least eight meetings, in addition to the time set aside for the religious celebration, if all the outlined sessions are used. An outline for eight meetings is given below. The mid-project revision and any of the outlined sessions can, of course, be omitted.

SAMPLE OUTLINE

Meeting 1—Commitment Service (see Appendix F) and Session I

Meeting 2—Session II

Meeting 3—Session III

Meeting 4—Plan the social action project

Meeting 5—Discuss ways to cope with negative aspects of the social action project; plan home devotions

Meeting 6—Plan and prepare for a religious celebration on the theme

   —Celebration

Meeting 7—Mid-project revision

Meeting 8—Evaluation

SOCIAL ACTION PROJECT SUGGESTIONS

There are many groups of people within the community with and for whom the youth group can act in faith and mirror God's faithfulness. Some of these include children who have few opportunities for developing a trusting relationship with someone older, children who are experiencing difficulties with schoolwork, and senior citizens and handicapped persons who find it difficult to get out to the grocery store or to run other errands. Here are three possible projects in faith with these groups of people: (1) Develop a trusting relationship with younger children in the community. In this program the members of the youth group adopt younger children as "brothers" and "sisters" and plan weekly shared activities with the little brothers and sisters. (2) For younger children who are experiencing some difficulties with schoolwork, organize a tutorial program in which members of the youth group would work on a one-to-one basis with younger children. (3) For senior citizens and handicapped persons, organize a service in which members of the youth group run errands for senior citizens and handicapped persons in the neighborhood.

SOME SUGGESTIONS FOR RESEARCHING THE PROJECTS

An informal survey of the neighborhood would help the group determine whether or not any of the three projects suggested above would be of use in the community. Such a survey would indicate whether, in fact, there are many children in the neighborhood who could benefit from and enjoy a big-brother or big-sister relationship, whether there are children experiencing difficulty with schoolwork, or whether there are elderly and handicapped persons in the neighborhood who need help in getting things from the grocery or in performing other tasks. Additional research and study might include the following:

1. Consult with teachers in local schools to determine which children might benefit most from a tutorial program such as the group proposes.

2. Determine which of these children would be willing to participate in a tutorial program.

3. Find out from the teachers how the youth can best help those children who are to be included in the program.

4. Role-play classroom situations to sensitize those who will be working in the program to the feelings which children who are having difficulties in school might experience and to how these feelings might be expressed.

5. Determine which elderly and handicapped persons in the neighborhood would like to have the errand service.

6. Devise a system in which errand runners, when they are asked to make purchases, can render a written accounting of the amount of money received, the amount spent on purchases, and the change (see "Coping with Negative Aspects" below).

7. Create role plays to sensitize those working on this social action project to the feelings which people who must be dependent on others to do things for them might experience and to how these feelings might be expressed.

COPING WITH NEGATIVE ASPECTS

All three of the suggested projects would require a lengthy commitment for members of the youth group. Thus, it is important before embarking on any of these projects to discuss seriously whether or not the group is willing to make such a commitment. If, for any reason, a sizable number of those in the group seem hesitant concerning the commitment required, it would be best to plan a project which can be completed within a shorter period of time.

There are several negative aspects which may surface if the group does decide to embark on any of the three suggested projects. Some of the youth may dislike working with the elderly or with children or may feel that they do not have the patience to work as tutors. If a substantial part of the group is committed to the project, however, "back-room" jobs can be found for those who would not be comfortable serving in front-line positions (see Appendix H).

Personality conflicts may arise between the youth and their little sisters or little brothers, between the youth and some of the children they are tutoring, or between the youth and some of the elderly or handicapped persons for whom they would be running errands. A frank discussion of each of the difficult situations, with the entire group participating, should be planned during the mid-project revision.

Conflicts over money may also come about in the errand service project. The potential for conflict, however, can perhaps be diminished with good advance planning. The following suggestions may prove helpful.

1. Only persons with proven honesty and ability to count change would be used as errand-runners in the project.

2. The amount of money which the errand runner could accept for any one errand could be limited.

3. A receipt booklet could be made up for the use of the errand runners. Each errand would involve using two sheets from the booklet and a sheet of carbon paper. When requested to run an errand, the errand runner would write out the amount given and possibly also a list of the items requested. The elderly person would sign the sheet and be given the duplicate copy which has been made with the carbon paper. At the store the errand runner would either ask the cashier to sign the cash register receipt, or, if there is no register receipt, write the amount of the purchase in the errand runner's receipt book and sign it. The errand runner would then give the cash register receipt to the person for whom he or she ran the errand or would show the amount of purchase and signature of the cashier in the receipt book.

4. The group might refuse to continue to run errands for those persons who have made more than a set number of complaints against several errand runners.

For additional suggestions on coping with negative aspects of the project, see Appendix H.

HOME DEVOTIONS

In addition to the biblical material and meditations given in the outlined session, these Bible passages may be useful for home devotions: Genesis 12:1-9; 17:1-8; 18:1-15; 21:1-8; 22:1-19; Psalms 36:5*b*; 89:1; 119:90*a*; Matthew 15:21-28; Mark 5:21-43; 9:14-29; Luke 7:1-10; 18:35-43; Galatians 3:7; Ephesians 3:14-19; 2 Timothy 2:13; Hebrews 10:23. Prayers from *The Book of Common Prayer* which are appropriate for this theme are the first prayer for Ascension Day, on p. 226, and Propers 25 and 26 on p. 235. For additional suggestions for home devotions, see Appendix I.

CELEBRATION

For general comments on using the Eucharist, or Holy Communion, for the celebration, see Appendix J. The service can stress the nature of faith as trust and willingness to risk, imaging God's faithfulness, and developing faith to sustain others and enable them to reach their goals. All of these topics are discussed in the outlined sessions for this unit.

MUSIC

In addition to the hymns suggested in Session I, Step 5, in this unit, "I Want Jesus to Walk with Me," "Walk Together, Children," "We Shall Overcome," and "Where He Leads Me, I Will Follow" are appropriate for this theme.

EVALUATION

See "Suggestions for Project Evaluation," Appendix L.

Unit on Community

Background

3

The wilderness, or desert, experience was of tremendous importance for the Israelites as a people. In this barren, hostile environment, where they were totally dependent on God, the Israelites came not only to know their limitations but also their worth both corporately and individually as a people of God. It was in the wilderness, too, that the Israelites were given the covenant, the agreement between God and the people which acknowledged God as the head of the community and which provided rules which, if kept, would enable the Israelites to enjoy in their society the conditions of love, freedom, justice, joy, and peace which God willed.

As Christians, we are still committed to a community of which God is the initiator and head. We are committed to a community where we are guided by the Holy Spirit to work in and with Christ toward the conditions which God wants for God's people. In Session I the youth will examine commitment to community as a prelude to working toward strengthening the intergenerational ties and commitments in the congregation, the Christian community of which they are members. Like the ancient Israelites, blacks have struggled through barren and hostile times here in America to come to some sense of their limitations and of their worth as a people. The youth look at this process in Session II. They then go on to try to determine what the needs and concerns of blacks are in the present and what they feel the goals and aspirations of blacks should be for the future. Session III involves a survey designed first to help the youth to discover what people in the congregation and in the community surrounding the church building see to be the needs, concerns, goals, and aspirations of black people. Secondly, the youth are to determine the commitments and actions necessary to deal with those expressed needs and aspirations. In Session IV the members of the group work together at different tasks, like the parts of the body, to produce a single product. Then they look at their several strengths and abilities and try to envision how, as members of the body of Christ, they can work together using their individual strengths for the benefit of the entire body and the continuation of the work of Christ in the world. The suggested projects provide an opportunity for continuing and extending the activities begun in the outlined sessions.

Make a Commitment

PURPOSE

To enable youth

—to examine the Garvey movement of the 1920s

—to view the covenant and Jesus' summary of the Law as commitments to a community with God as its head

—to formulate and make a commitment to God, to one another, and across the generations in their community

OUTLINE OF SESSION

Step 1—Garvey and the UNIA: A Creative Drama

Step 2—God and Community

Step 3—Our Commitment to Community

Step 4—Follow-Up (and Formal Commitment)

Step 5—Activity: How Am I Related to You?

(Step 6—Evaluation)

Step 1—Garvey and the UNIA: A Creative Drama

This session begins with a creative drama based on the life of Marcus Garvey. A creative drama does not require that the players learn any lines before they begin the play. Instead, they simply listen to a story, decide on the scenes necessary to portray the drama, and create appropriate dialogue and action as they act out the story.

1. Read or tell the following story of Marcus Garvey to the group.

2. Have the group decide on the scenes necessary to portray the story (some are suggested below).

3. Assign parts to members of the group. If you like, have someone act as narrator to fill in important details in the story which cannot be shown in the scenes.

4. Have the members of the group act out the story, creating the dialogue and action as they go along.

Marcus Garvey

Marcus Garvey was a black Jamaican born in 1887. When he was a child, Garvey noticed that black people took no part in the government of Jamaica. He asked his mother, "Where is the black man's government?" but she was unable to answer him.

As a young man, Garvey traveled to Latin America and London, studying the conditions of blacks in those places. In 1914 he returned to Jamaica to form the United Negro Improvement Association (UNIA). By 1916 Garvey had opened a branch of the UNIA in Harlem.

The aim of the UNIA was to free, save, and better the conditions of blacks everywhere and to promote a sense of unity, self-reliance, and pride in the race. The Association sponsored a newspaper and had auxiliaries for youth and divisions such as the Black Cross Nurses and the African Legion. It began black-owned economic enterprises, the most prominent of which was the Black Star Steamship Line. At Liberty Hall, the UNIA headquarters, the organization provided religious services, concerts, and dances for its members and free lunches and temporary lodging for any blacks who were unemployed. In frequent speeches and through his newspaper, *The Negro World,* Garvey appealed to black newspaper publishers and owners to stop carrying skin bleaching and hair straightening advertisements and asked black mothers to provide black dolls for their little girls to play with. In guidelines to the UNIA, Garvey advised the members of the organization to work hard, to save all they could, and to vote in elections as the Association directed for the good of the cause.

Perhaps the most visible reminder of the UNIA in our midst today is the red, black, and green liberation flag. The Association adopted that flag in 1920 at one of its annual conventions, which, at the height of the Garvey movement, were held at Madison Square Garden.

The UNIA was best known for its Back to Africa movement. Critics of the UNIA thought that Garvey intended to undertake the economically impossible task of sending all black Americans to Africa. But Garvey's widow has said that he intended to transport only technicians and specialists who would be particularly helpful in creating a strong black nation as a refuge and homeland somewhere on the continent.

Garvey's critics also criticized the orders of nobility created for the outstanding members of the UNIA, the parades in which its uniformed members marched through the streets of New York City, and Garvey's apparent friendliness with the leaders of the Ku Klux Klan. Garvey publicly met with the leaders of the Klan and congratulated them because he believed that the Klan acted out the hatred and prejudice which all white Americans felt but which others were too polite or cultured to express in violence.

Black leaders of the period, such as W. E. B. Du Bois, James Weldon Johnson, and A. Philip Randolph, denounced Garvey also because he had declared that these leaders had no program and were controlled by the white philanthropists who supported their organizations. In the UNIA, Garvey had consistently refused contributions from whites and had even made stocks for the Black Star Lines available only to members of the Association, which was restricted to blacks.

Finally, the other black leaders urged that the government bring Garvey to trial over a case of mail fraud based on his stock-selling venture. At the trial, the finances of the Black Star Line were seen to be badly tangled. Even though Garvey could, undoubtedly, appeal to the masses of black people and articulate their needs, he was less able as a businessman. In 1925, Garvey was convicted and sentenced to the Atlanta Penitentiary. During his time there, he continued to discuss with visitors his hopes and plans for the race. After his release, he was deported to England, where he died. However, many of the ideals he stood for—black self-reliance and solidarity throughout the world—are still important to black people today.

Some Suggested Scenes

- Garvey as a child with his mother
- UNIA delegates parade in uniform to Madison Square Garden to listen to a speech by Garvey
- The black leaders discuss Garvey
- Garvey in prison talking with a visitor

Step 2—God and Community

Following the creative drama, have the youth discuss Garvey and the UNIA.

1. "What were Garvey's goals—the goals of the UNIA—for black people?" (To free, save, and better the conditions of blacks everywhere and to promote a sense of unity, self-reliance, and pride in the race.)

2. "What were some of the commitments Garvey suggested that his followers make in order to realize these goals?" (To provide financial backing for black economic enterprises, to work hard and save money, to vote in elections as the Association directed, to buy black dolls for their children, and to stop using skin bleaches and hair straighteners.)

Summarize the following biblical background for the group:

Living together in community and trying to reach goals which are of importance to everyone always demands that the members of the community make certain commitments. In fact, it is often in deciding upon the commitments which they must make that the members of the group discover who they are as a community. In biblical times, when God brought the Israelite people out of slavery in Egypt, they had no sense of nationhood or unity and common purpose. It was only after they had agreed at Mount Sinai to make a covenant with God that the Israelites began to understand who they were as a people. They knew that their God was concerned for their welfare, merciful, and compassionate since God had delivered them from slavery and had provided for their needs as they journeyed through the wilderness.

In the covenant the Israelites agreed on a common goal: to acknowledge God as the King and head of their community and the One whose will should rule them all. The Commandments which God gave them as part of the covenant were commitments to love the God with whom they wished to unite themselves and to imitate God's mercy, concern, and compassion in their dealings with one another. By keeping these Commandments, the Israelites would be able to realize the community, or kingdom, which God wished to establish on earth: a kingdom of love, freedom, justice, peace, and well-being for all. (For biblical descriptions of the kingdom, see Isaiah 11:1-9; 61:1-3; 65:21-25; and Ezekiel 34:23-31.) In such a community as this, all would realize their full human potential to live as holy beings as God is holy (see Leviticus 11:45).

But the Israelites could not keep their commitments to God and to one another. As faith in God and love of God failed, the strong began to take advantage of the weak, and it was thus impossible for many to realize their full human potential or for the community as a whole to live the life of God's kingdom.

In the person of Jesus Christ, God came to the Israelites and to all people to free both oppressors and oppressed from all that would prevent them from realizing their full human potential and to initiate the kingdom of God. In the commitment which Christ asked of those who would follow—i.e., in the summary of the Law (Matthew 22:34-40)—all the commandments of the covenant were summed up. Furthermore, God gave to the church, the community that had been formed by God, Christ's own Spirit, the Spirit of God to enable us to be truly human, to be holy as God is holy (see John 15:1-17; Romans 8:9; 1 Peter 1:15-16). Led by the Spirit, the church, which is the Body of Christ, continues to work in and with Christ toward the realization of the kingdom which God wills.

Step 3—Our Commitment to Community

1. Comment: "We have looked at the goals of one group, or community, the UNIA. And we have seen the commitments which members of that group would have to make to realize their goals. We have just heard in general something of the goals and commitments of the people of God. All of us, as members of the congregation, are members of the community of the people of God in this place.

2. "What do you think should be our goals for life

together in this community? How should children, young people, adults, and the elderly relate to one another? What should be the goals of this group in relation to God? What should they be in relation to other age groups in the congregation? What should the goals be concerning ourselves and one another? How do you feel the other age groups should relate to those in this group?"

Have one person act as recorder and write on the board or on newsprint the ideas that are given by the group. After all the goals have been given and discussed by the youth, have them formulate tentatively the commitments that would be necessary to make to God, to themselves, to one another, to the younger children, to the adults, and to the elderly to reach those goals toward which they would like to work.

Step 4—Follow-Up (and Formal Commitment)

Have the youth decide which members of their group will meet with the other generational groups—the younger children, the adults, and the elderly—or their representatives to review and negotiate the goals and commitments which the group has outlined. In these meetings it should be determined whether the other age groups can agree to the relationship which the youth have proposed, or whether the goals set by the youth will have to be adjusted to suit the needs of the other age groups in the congregation. Since this task may prove to be difficult in some instances, it may be helpful if an adult leader can plan to be present at these meetings. Once goals and commitments which are mutually satisfactory to the youth and the other groups have been agreed upon, representatives of all the age groups can plan a commitment service to formalize their agreements.

Step 5—Activity: How Am I Related to You?

1. Have the members of the group cut out of newspapers and magazines pictures of children, youth, adults, and the elderly.

2. Have them paste the pictures on a large sheet of poster board with ribbons running from the pictures of one age group to another.

3. Attach a pad of paper and pencil to the board, and post it in a prominent place in the church building.

4. Have the youth ask the members of the congregation to write on the pad how they think members of each age group should relate to the others.

(Step 6—Evaluation)

To evaluate the session with the group, see the suggestions given in Appendix E.

Desert Road

PURPOSE

To enable youth

—to see the wilderness (desert) experience as a maturing one for the Israelite people

—to explore some desert experiences for blacks in the United States and some of the insights gained from those experiences

—to envision some of the needs, concerns, aspirations, and goals of blacks for the future

—to commit themselves and their people to God for the future

OUTLINE OF SESSION

Step 1—In the Wilderness (Desert)

Step 2—A Highway in the Desert

Step 3—Visioning

Step 4—Prayer: "Into Thy Hands . . ."

Step 5—Song

Step 6—Activity: What Do We Need? Where Are We Going?

(Step 7—Evaluation)

Step 1—In the Wilderness (Desert)

Summarize the following commentary for the group: When the Israelite people left Egypt, after God had freed them from slavery there, they wandered for a long time in a desert area called the wilderness. It was while they were in this harsh environment, where they had to depend entirely on God, that they came to know more about their God and more about themselves as a people. Because God had delivered them from slavery and provided them miraculously with food and water in the barren wilderness, the Israelites came to know that God was concerned about their welfare and is merciful and compassionate. Since God's actions had taken place within their own history, the Israelites knew that their God is one who acts in history. And since God had commanded their obedient cooperation in some of these actions—at the Passover rite, when gathering the manna, and when obtaining water from a rock in the wilderness, for example—they knew that God is a God who wills that human beings cooperate in shaping their history. Most important, what the Israelites came to know about God during their wilderness period, they came to know through their own *experience* of God at that time.

The Israelites also came to understand more about who they were as a people and how they related to God during their desert experience. Whether they realized it at the time or whether it became apparent to them later as they reflected on this period, the Israelites came to see themselves as a disobedient, argumentative, and faithless people (see Exodus 32; Numbers 11:1-6; etc.). But in addition to recognizing their limitations, the Israelites came to see that they had worth—both as individuals and as a group. In both cases their worth stemmed not so much from themselves and what they had done as from God. The Israelites had worth as a people not because they were a large and mighty nation or had done anything great but simply because God loved them (Deuteronomy 7:7-8). Because God loved them, God had especially chosen them as a people and had given them the mission to be a holy people, a kingdom of priests through whom the rest of the world would be blessed (Exodus 19:6). As the Israelites came to work out how they should behave as the people of God, they discovered that the individual simply by virtue of being one of God's people had certain worth and could expect certain rights because of this worth. According to the covenant, or agreement, which the Israelites made with God, it was God's will that each one of the people have, for example, the right to justice within the society (Leviticus 19:15) and the food necessary to sustain life (Deuteronomy 24:19-22).

For the Israelites, the years spent in the desert, or wilderness, were especially important for the formation and understanding of themselves as a people and for their growth and development. Even after the experience was long past, prophets such as Hosea longed for a return to the desert conditions, for a return to a time when the people would be totally dependent on God, so that Israel could again appreciate that all that it had and all that it was was a gift from God. For these prophets and for many others the desert stood for a place where people found God and came to know who they were in relationship to God. Jesus himself went into the desert before embarking on his mission, and many early Christian monks and nuns spent their lives in the desert in a continual search for a better knowledge of God and themselves.

For blacks in the United States there have been many periods which were like desert periods, many times when conditions for living were so harsh that they were forced to depend wholly on God for their survival. Obviously, slavery was one of these periods. Not only were blacks during slavery completely deprived of the right to control their own destiny, often treated harshly, and separated by slave sales from other members of their families, but they were also told by white slave owners and preachers that they had been destined by God to be the servants of other peoples. Although slavery was abolished at the end of the Civil War, conditions for blacks, after initially improving, worsened until by the 1920s blacks were legally segregated from whites and provided with inferior facilities in all areas of the South. Discrimination against blacks flourished in the North; mob violence against blacks was common throughout the country. Furthermore, many, both black and white, were convinced that blacks were innately inferior to whites. Although in the 1960s blacks obtained access to many of the facilities from which they had been excluded and began to enjoy some measure of equality and opportunity, many perceptive people realized that very few blacks had the power to shape their own lives or the freedom to determine their own destiny. They saw that most blacks were still at the mercy of those who control the means of production for their employment, at the mercy of those who could control prices in the housing market to determine where they live, at the mercy of those who hold political and especially economic power in the society. In the midst of harsh, desertlike conditions, blacks in the United States, like the ancient Israelites in the wilderness, have gradually come to a clearer understanding of their God, their own worth and limitations, and their mission as God's people.

Step 2—A Highway in the Desert

1. Divide the youth into small groups.

2. Assign each of the groups one of the selections below.

3. Ask the members to discuss the selection in the group and decide on the answers to the questions following the selection.

4. Reassemble the entire body and have a spokesperson from each group present the selection, the discussion, and the group's conclusions.

Selection 1

From "Richard Allen and Absalom Jones Speak Out Against Slavery," in Alfred E. Cain, ed., *The Winding Road to Freedom* (Yonkers: Educational Heritage, Inc., 1965), pp. 64-65. *This article was written in 1794.*

"The judicious part of mankind will think it unreasonable, that a superior good conduct is looked for, from our race, by those who stigmatize us as men, whose baseness is incurable, and may therefore be held in a state of servitude, that a merciful man would not deem a beast to; yet you try what you can to prevent our rising from the state of barbarism, you represent us to be in, but we can tell you, from a degree of experience, that a black man, although reduced to the most abject state human nature is capable of, short of real madness, can think, reflect, and feel injuries, although it may not be with the same degree of keen resentment and revenge, that you who have been and are our great oppressors, would manifest if reduced to the pitiable condition of a slave. . . .

"We do not wish to make you angry, but excite your attention to consider, how hateful slavery is in the sight of that God, who hath destroyed kings and princes, for their oppression of the poor slaves; Pharaoh and his princes with the posterity of King Saul, were destroyed by the protector and avenger of slaves. Would you not suppose the Israelites to be utterly unfit for freedom, and that it was impossible for them to attain to any degree of excellence? Their history shews how slavery had debased their spirits. Men must be wilfully blind and extremely partial, that cannot see the contrary effects of liberty and slavery upon the mind of man; we freely confess the vile habits often acquired in a state of servitude, are not easily thrown off; the example of the Israelite shews, who with all that Moses could do to reclaim them from it, still continued in their former habits more or less; and why will you look for better from us? Why will you look for grapes from thorns, or figs from thistles? It is in our posterity enjoying the same privileges with your own, that you ought to look for better things. . . .

"God himself hath pleaded their cause, he hath from time to time raised up instruments for that purpose, sometimes mean and contemptible in your sight; at other times he hath used such as it hath pleased him with whom you have not thought it beneath your dignity to contend, many add to your numbers, until the princes shall come forth from Egypt and Ethiopia stretch out her hand unto God."

How does the statement show that blacks had come to know God on their own? How does it show that blacks had come to appreciate their own worth?

Selection 2

From "Resolutions of the N.A.A.C.P., 1919," in Herbert Aptheker, ed., *A Documentary History of the Negro People in the United States, 1910-1932* (Secaucus, N.J.: The Citadel Press, 1973), p. 247. Copyright 1973 by Herbert Aptheker. Used by permission of Citadel Press.

"Looking to the achievement of the foregoing ends, we declare the platform of the National Association for the Advancement of Colored People to be the following:

1. A vote for every colored man and woman on the same terms as for white men and women.

2. An equal chance to acquire the kind of education

that will enable the colored citizen everywhere wisely to use this vote.

3. A fair trial in the courts for all crimes of which he is accused by judges in whose election he has participated without discrimination because of race.
4. A right to sit upon the jury which passes judgement upon him.
5. Defense against lynching and burning at the hands of mobs.
6. Equal service on railroad and other public carriers. This to mean sleeping car service, dining car service, Pullman service, at the same cost and upon the same terms as other passengers.
7. Equal right to the use of public parks, libraries and other community services for which he is taxed.
8. An equal chance for a livelihood in public and private employment.
9. The abolition of color-hyphenation and the substitution of 'straight Americanism.'"

How does this selection show that blacks had come to appreciate their own worth?

Selection 3

Langston Hughes, "I, Too," copyright 1926 by Alfred A. Knopf, Inc., and renewed 1954 by Langston Hughes. Reprinted from *Selected Poems of Langston Hughes*, by Langston Hughes, by permission of Alfred A. Knopf, Inc.

I, too, sing America.

I am the darker brother.
They send me to eat in the kitchen
When company comes,
But I laugh,
And eat well,
And grow strong.

Tomorrow,
I'll be at the table
When company comes.
Nobody'll dare
Say to me,
"Eat in the kitchen,"
Then.

Besides,
They'll see how beautiful I am
And be ashamed—

I, too, am America.

How does the selection show that blacks had come to appreciate their own worth?

Selection 4

From "A Theological Purpose Programmatic Statement," published by the Episcopal Commission for Black Ministries, 1978.

In the promise and challenge of freedom in Jesus Christ, Christians experience a vital, dynamic relationship with the Holy Spirit of the one true living God. To know God is to be both liberated and liberating. To love God and to love all humankind as we love ourselves is to share with our Messiah, Jesus, both celebration of and the struggle for freedom from all forms of sin and bondage. . . .

. . . we are called, individually and corporately, to be actively engaged in transforming the ecclesiastical, social, and political systems which intentionally or unconsciously impede our full participation in the liberation to which Jesus calls us. . . .

God speaks to us as free persons, redeemed from bondage by the life, death, and resurrection of Jesus the Messiah. We understand that liberation is not only an eschatological hope but also a constant challenge to resist external structures and internal weaknesses that perpetuate the sin of oppression or encourage the sin of submission.

We recognize and seek to analyze more clearly the forces of racism, paternalism, cultural subjugation, economic exploitation, and institutionalized dehumanization which wreak havoc upon community, family, and personal lives. We recommit ourselves to challenge these forces of wickedness in high places, prayerfully mindful of the enormity of these tasks.

Yet we are also mindful of our own sinfulness and our need for active repentance. We repent and actively seek to rectify such failings as dependency, mimicry of our oppressors, narrowness of vision, vapidity in religious life, avoidance of social involvement, isolation from fellow believers, slackness in propagation of our faith, failure to exercise our fullest potential competence, and submission to dehumanizing power.

How does this statement show that blacks have come to know God? Have come to know their own limitations? Have come to realize their mission in relationship to God?

Step 3—Visioning

Comment: "Now that we have looked a bit at the black American past, let us think in terms of the present and the future."

Ask the group members to decide what they think the greatest needs and concerns of black people are at present and what their goals and aspirations for the future should be. Have the recorder write these on the board or on newsprint.

Step 4—Prayer: "Into Thy Hands . . ."

1. Have the youth imagine that they are in the presence of Christ. (Pause)

2. Have them commit the needs and concerns, goals and aspirations expressed in Step 3 into God's hands and promise to wait and see how God would have them individually and/or as a group work toward the goals and aspirations.

Step 5—Song

Sing "He's Got the Whole World in His Hands," "We've Come This Far by Faith," or some other appropriate song.

Step 6—Activity: What Do We Need? Where Are We Going?

Have the youth make posters illustrating the needs, concerns, goals, and aspirations they expressed in Step 3. Have them place the posters in prominent places in the church building and invite the other members of the congregation to dialogue with them concerning what they think the needs and concerns of blacks are at present and what their goals and aspirations should be for the future.

(Step 7—Evaluation)

To evaluate the session with the group, see the suggestions given in Appendix E.

What Do We Need? Where Do We Want to Go?

PURPOSE

To enable youth
- —to discover what members of the congregation and of the community surrounding the church building feel are the needs and concerns and what should be the goals and aspirations of blacks in the United States over the next five years
- —to trace the origins of Christian commitments to community with God as head
- —to explore the commitments necessary to deal with the expressed needs, concerns, goals, and aspirations of black people

OUTLINE OF SESSION

Step 1—Survey: Let's Find Out
Step 2—God and Community
Step 3—What Are We Willing to Give?
Step 4—Prayer: "Into Thy Hands . . ."
(Step 5—Evaluation)

Step 1—Survey: Let's Find Out

This session involves a survey for which some advance preparation is necessary. The survey is designed to determine (1) what people in the congregation and in the community surrounding the church building feel to be the most pressing needs and concerns of black people in the United States and (2) what they feel should be their goals and aspirations over the next five years. People in the community surrounding the church building could be interviewed on Saturdays at local grocery stores, playgrounds and other recreational facilities, and at other places in the neighborhood where many people gather. Members of the congregation could be interviewed on a Sunday after the worship service. Remind the members of the group to include young people in the survey as well as adults and senior citizens. Have them interview one another before they begin the general survey so as to obtain both the necessary data from the youth of the congregation and to give the members of the group an opportunity to practice their interviewing techniques. In preparation for the practice interviews and the general survey, mimeograph enough copies of the list of questions so that there will be one copy to record the answers for each person interviewed (see the suggested questionnaire below). Hand out the questionnaires, and come to an agreement with the youth on when the survey will be conducted and at what session the completed questionnaires will be discussed.

A Suggested Questionnaire

1. What do you think black people in this community (that is, the community around the church building) need most?
2. What do you think most people in this community are most concerned about?
3. What do you think are the most important things that black people should be working toward in the next five years?

After the interview, fill in the following information: Approximate age of the person interviewed:

—under 20   —20-64 years   —65 or over

—male   —female

—member of the congregation   —non-member

After the youth have conducted the survey, have them bring the completed questionnaires to the session. Have one member of the group act as recorder while another person reads the answers from the questionnaires.

1. On newsprint or on the board have the recorder list in separate columns the needs, concerns, and proposed goals that were mentioned by members of the congregation.
2. If the same item was listed by more than one person, have the recorder keep track of the number of people who mentioned it.
3. Note, also, how often the item was mentioned by persons under 20, by persons between 20 and 64 years of age, by persons 65 or older, by males, and by females.
4. On separate sheets of newsprint or on another part of the board, have the recorder list the information in 1-3 above for those who are not members of the congregation.
5. Have the group look at the results of the questionnaires to see whether or not the needs, concerns, and goals or aspirations:
   - (a) of those who are not members of the congregation are the same as those who are members.
   - (b) of those who are under 20 years of age are the same as those who are 20-64 or those who are 65 or older.
   - (c) of the men are the same as those of the women.

Step 2—God and Community

Give a summary of the following:
In the results of the questionnaire, we see different

opinions of the needs, concerns, goals, and aspirations of our community. In order to gain a perspective on our task as a specifically Christian group, in relation to our community and their expressed concerns and goals, we need now to review some biblical teaching and background.

One of God's first and most decisive acts in the formation of a people especially consecrated to divine service came about when the Israelite people were delivered from slavery and oppression in Egypt. Although we say that God delivered the Israelites, the people who came out of Egypt were not of one race (see Exodus 12:38) and were by no means united as to where they were going or what they should be doing. They went together into the desert, though, to worship a God whom they didn't know very well but whom they believed was active in history and in the affairs of human beings because this God had just delivered them from slavery. As they journeyed through the desert, where food and water are scarce, the Israelites came to know that God is merciful and compassionate, for they were continually provided with all that was necessary for life.

At Mount Sinai, still in the desert, when the Israelites assented to making a covenant with God, they began to take the first steps toward becoming a united people, a true community. The Israelites saw the covenant as an agreement with God which acknowledged God as the Head and true King of their people, as One whose will should unite and rule them all. By carrying out the commandments included in the covenant, they would eventually take on God's personality and develop their full human potential to live together as holy beings, just as God is holy (Leviticus 11:45). The commandments were particularly geared toward loving the God with whom the Israelites wished to unite themselves and toward imitating God's mercy, concern, and compassion in their dealings with one another. But the Israelites could not keep the covenant they had made and frequently sinned. Because they did not love God in the total way that was commanded (Deuteronomy 6:5), they were unable to imitate God's mercy, concern, and compassion in their dealings with one another. They, in fact, began to oppress one another and thus prevent many in their community from realizing their full human potential and from sharing in the life or love, freedom, justice, peace, and well-being which God wants for all the people.

Hundreds of years after God had liberated the Israelite people from the bonds of slavery and oppression in Egypt and had initiated a community with them in the covenant, God came in the person of Jesus Christ to liberate them and all others from sin and from all that would prevent their full development as human beings, and to establish God's kingdom. The community which Christ formed, the community of the members of his body, the church, is also one with God as Head or King. In the community of the church, also, it is God's will which should rule. In addition to the expression of this will in the two commandments which Jesus Christ gave us, to love God and to love one another (Matthew 22:34-40), the church and its members are given Christ's own Spirit, the Spirit of God, to enable them to be loving, to be truly human, to be holy as God is holy (see John 15:1-17; Romans 8:9; 1 Peter 1:15-16).

To be truly human, to be holy as God is holy, is to love all humankind as God loves and, thus, to share with Christ the task of liberating all, both those within the church and those outside of it, from everything that would prevent them from reaching their full human potential. By sharing in this work, the church joins with its Lord in forming the community, the kingdom of love, freedom, justice, peace, and total well-being which God wills. In considering the needs and concerns, aspirations and goals both of the members of the congregation and of those in the surrounding neighborhood, our main objective, as Christians, is to share with Christ in this work of liberation and of bringing into being Christ's kingdom where there is love, freedom, justice, peace, and total well-being for all.

Step 3—What Are We Willing to Give?

1. Have the group look again at the results of the survey.

2. Which of the expressed needs, concerns, goals, and aspirations are most important for helping those around us develop their full human potential and for bringing about the kind of community which God wills?

3. If those needs, etc., have been expressed largely by only one of the groups surveyed (for example, those outside the congregation rather than those in it, or the elderly rather than the youth or adults), how could we go about enlisting the aid of the other groups in working toward them? (In some cases, others may not be aware of the felt needs or aspirations of other groups.)

4. List in separate columns the ATTITUDES, ACTIONS, and COMMITMENTS that would be necessary to deal with these needs, concerns, goals, and aspirations.

5. What attitudes, actions, and commitments would this group have to make to deal with one or more of these needs, concerns, goals, and aspirations?

If you wish, the group may make a plan of action to

deal with one or more of these needs, concerns, or goals and to enlist, if necessary, the aid of other groups to work with them in carrying out their plan.

Step 4—Prayer: "Into Thy Hands . . ."

1. Have the members of the group imagine that they are in the presence of Christ. (Pause)

2. As the following verses are read, have the group imagine what would be happening in the community, how it would look if these conditions were fulfilled.

"Let justice roll down like waters, and righteousness like an ever-flowing stream" (Amos 5:24, RSV). (Pause)

"'Set at liberty those who are oppressed'" (Luke 4:18*b*, RSV). (Pause)

"'Love one another, as I have loved you'" (John 15:12*b*, RSV). (Pause)

"Steadfast love and faithfulness will meet; righteousness and peace will kiss each other" (Psalm 85:10, RSV). (Pause)

3. Have the group members imagine how the atittudes, actions, and commitments which they have outlined might contribute to bringing into being these desired conditions. (Pause)

4. Have them hand to Christ the attitudes, actions, and commitments which they have outlined along with their image of the new conditions which these attitudes, actions, and commitments might help to bring about. (Pause)

5. Have each person ask Christ to change the image, if necessary, where it does not truly represent Christ's will, either now or as work continues. (Pause)

6. Have the members of the group commend themselves and one another, the community, and the attitudes, actions, and commitments they have outlined into God's hands. (Pause)

Allow those who wish to share and discuss their meditation with the group to do so.

(Step 5—Evaluation)

To evaluate the session with the group, see the suggestions given in Appendix E.

Many Parts, One Body

PURPOSE

To enable youth

—to work together at different tasks to produce a single product

—to see themselves as different parts of the same Body

—to appreciate one another's strengths and abilities

—to envision how they can use their many strengths and abilities to work for themselves and others

OUTLINE OF SESSION

PART A

Step 1—Cooperative Cake Bake

PART B

Step 2—Many Parts, One Body

Step 3—Likes and Strengths

Step 4—Prayer: Round-Robin Thanksgiving

(Step 5—Eat Cake, Clean Up, and Evaluate)

Part A of this session involves a cake bake and should take place where there are baking facilities and enough room for all the members of your group to participate in the exercise. Have ready the ingredients and utensils necessary for baking a simple cake, a simple cake recipe, a rudimentary knowledge of how to bake a cake, and lots of patience. If you use butter or margarine, don't forget to set it out ahead of time.

Since Step 3 in this session is only effective where members of the group know one another fairly well, this session is recommended only for groups who have met together on previous occasions.

PART A: Step 1—Cooperative Cake Bake

Divide the group into several small groups. Each small group will be assigned different tasks necessary for baking a cake. The cake making could be divided among the groups as follows:

Group 1—Turn on the oven; grease and flour the cake or cupcake tins.

Group 2—Cream butter or margarine; measure and add sugar and vanilla to butter or margarine.

Group 3—Beat the egg(s); add egg(s) to margarine-sugar-vanilla mixture.

Group 4—Sift and measure flour; put measured salt and baking powder with flour in sifter to be added to other ingredients.

Group 5—Measure milk; after Group 6 has added some of the dry ingredients to the margarine-sugar-vanilla-egg mixture, alter-nate with Group 6 in adding milk to mixture.

Group 6—Add dry ingredients to margarine-sugar-vanilla-egg mixture, alternating with Group 5, who will add the milk; beat after every addition.

Group 7—Pour the cake batter into prepared cake or cupcake tins, put the tins in the oven, time the baking, and test the cake or cupcakes to see when they are done.

As members of each group finish their tasks, they may watch the others as they complete the process. After the cake is in the oven, continue the session.

PART B: Step 2—Many Parts, One Body

1. Begin Step 2 by commenting on how all the members of the group have worked together as if they were one person. Even though different people performed different tasks, they all worked together to accomplish one objective.

2. Have the members of the group turn to 1 Corinthians 12:4-12 and Ephesians 4:11-12.

3. Discuss how these passages apply to what was done in Step 1.

4. Give a summary of the following:

Each of us has been given certain gifts by God. We can find indications of what gifts God has given each of us by looking at our individual preferences, the things we like to do, and our strengths, the things we do well. The gifts that God has given us are not just for us to enjoy for ourselves. They are for building up the church, the body of Christ. That is, God has given us gifts to enable us to minister to one another and together to continue the ministry which Jesus Christ carried out when he was on earth. That ministry can be described in several different ways. It can be described as a ministry of liberation, a willingness to struggle as our Lord did, with and on behalf of ourselves and other human beings to free us and them from all that would prevent us from reaching our full human potential. (See Jesus' description of his work in Luke 4:18-21, which is, itself, largely a quote from Isaiah 61:1-2, a description of the work of the Messiah.) It can be described as a ministry of reconciliation, whereby Christ through his body, the church, enables us humans to resolve or reconcile the conflicts within ourselves, between ourselves and others, and between ourselves and God (see 2 Corinthians 5:15-20). This ministry can be described in terms of Christ's ongoing work of ushering in the rule of God on earth, of bringing into being that kingdom and time when love, freedom, peace, justice, joy, and well-being exist for all. (In allegorical terms Ezekiel 34:23-31; Isaiah 11:1-9; and 65:21-25 describe these conditions in the kingdom, which Jesus says in Matthew 4:17, Luke 11:20, and in other passages is at hand, or has come, with his coming.) Although we know that complete liberation, reconciliation, and the fullness of the rule of God on earth cannot be brought about solely through our efforts, as Christians we can and must work in and with Christ toward these goals. And each of us can contribute to this work in different ways.

Let us first look at our individual preferences and strengths. Then let us see how we can use these preferences and strengths as a group to do things together that we would enjoy and to minister to one another and to others in the congregation and in the larger community.

PART B: Step 3—Likes and Strengths

1. Have each person take a sheet of newsprint and write his or her name at the top of it with a crayon or a Magic Marker.

2. Ask each person to make two columns on the sheet and to list in one column the things he or she likes and in the other his or her strengths—the things he or she can do well.

3. When the sheets are finished, mount them around the room with masking tape.

4. Have the members of the group go around the room adding to the sheets strengths which they have noticed in the person whose sheet it is.

5. When all have finished going around the room, have the group gather where they can see all of the sheets.

6. Read, or have someone else read, through each sheet. Be sure to allow the person whose sheet is being read to react to (accept or deny) the strengths which others have observed and added to his or her list. Point out in what way the strengths listed can help others. (For example, a person who has listed "makes friends easily" can help others who don't have this skill to learn it.)

7. When all sheets have been read, use these questions for discussion:

Judging from the items listed by everyone in the "likes" column on the sheets, what sorts of things might we enjoy doing together as a group?

What are some of the needs of the congregation and the community surrounding the church building?

Judging from the things we have listed on our sheets as "likes" and "strengths," what sorts of things could we do as a group to minister to one or more of the needs of the congregation and/or the community?

8. If you wish, you may help the group put together a plan of action for ministering to one or more of the needs of the congregation and/or the community.

PART B: Step 4—Prayer: Round-Robin Thanksgiving

1. Have the members of the group form a circle.

2. Have each person thank God for the person on his or her right and for one or more of his or her strengths and/or likes. (Be sure to include the leader or leaders.)

3. Close the prayer with thanksgiving for the group and for their collective strengths and likes.

(PART B: Step 5—Eat Cake, Clean Up, and Evaluate)

Eat the cake or cupcakes either plain or iced. You can divide the group into small groups again, if you wish, to clean up the kitchen. (To evaluate the session with the members of the group, see the suggestions given in Appendix E.)

A Long-Term Project: Doing Something About Community

God's Revelation: "[Ye] . . . in time past were not a people, but are now the people of God" (1 Peter 2:10a); "We are members of his body, of his flesh, and of his bones. We are members one of another" (Ephesians 5:30; 4:25b).

Our Response: What is it to be black people of God in this place? What is it to be members of Christ's body, flesh and bones, and members one of another?

The long-term project for this unit will cover at least nine meetings, in addition to the time set aside for religious celebration, if all the preceding outlined sessions are used. An outline for the nine meetings is given below. The mid-project revision and any of the outlined sessions in the unit can, of course, be omitted.

SAMPLE OUTLINE

Meeting 1—Commitment Service (see Appendix F) and Session I

Meeting 2—Session II

Meeting 3—Session III

Meeting 4—Session IV

Meeting 5—Plan the social action project

Meeting 6—Discuss ways to cope with negative aspects of the social action project; plan home devotions

Meeting 7—Plan and prepare for a religious celebration on the theme

—Celebration

Meeting 8—Mid-project revision

Meeting 9—Evaluation

A RETREAT ON COMMUNITY

Several of the sessions above will have to be adapted if they are to be used in a retreat. For example, Session III and Step 4 in Session I could be deferred until after the retreat. If cooking facilities are not available, Part A in Session IV could involve some other cooperative task (for example, printing covers for the Sunday celebration, with Group I designing the covers, Group 2 cutting the potatoes for potato prints, and Group 3 doing the actual printing). The planning for the social action project, which would take place at the retreat, would necessarily be preliminary in nature without the results of the survey in Session III, especially if a project which goes beyond the work in that session is decided upon by the group.

SOCIAL ACTION PROJECT SUGGESTIONS

There are several possible projects on this theme. Social action projects for promoting a sense of community grow out of Session I and might involve intergenerational interaction or exchange. In one such project shut-ins in the congregation might construct quiet games for the use of the children and youth in recreational programs at the church. In exchange, the youth of the congregation would provide visits to the shut-ins with scrapbooks, slide shows, or movies and accounts of events which have taken place in the congregation, the community, and the city. Another such social action project might involve the youth with substitute grandparents. Members of the group would choose senior citizens in the congregation or community as their substitute grandmother or grandfather and the "grandparent" and "grandchild" would invite one another to outings, meals, etc.

Another type of project might be an extension of Sessions II and III and would involve work on those needs, concerns, goals, and aspirations of the congregation and the community which have the potential for bringing about the kind of community God wills.

SOME SUGGESTIONS FOR RESEARCHING THE PROJECTS
For a Shut-In–Youth Interchange

• Make an informal survey to determine how many and which shut-ins in the congregation and perhaps in nearby congregations might want to be involved in the interchange.

• Determine from a survey of the children and youth of the congregation and surrounding community which quiet games they enjoy which the shut-ins could make and how many sets of these games might be necessary.

• Determine from a survey of the shut-ins which activities in the congregation, community, or city each person might particularly want included in the scrapbooks, slide shows, or movies for his or her visit.

For Substitute Grandparents

• Little research is necessary for this project.

For Work Concerning the Needs, Concerns, Goals, and Aspirations of Blacks for the Future

Research would depend on the specific needs, concerns, goals and aspirations identified. However, hearings held by the Urban Bishops Coalition identified several issues of common concern for urban blacks. That group will be involved in planning work on parish, diocesan, and national levels in the Episcopal Church on these issues. A project for the group might well be tied into local work which has already been planned or is in progress. A report of the hearings held by the Urban Bishops Coalition and summary of their recommendations for action is published in *To Hear and to Heed* (Cincinnati: Forward Movement Publications, 1978). Information concerning projects which this group might undertake would be available from any of the diocesan headquarters listed on the front and back covers of the report.

COPING WITH NEGATIVE ASPECTS

Personality conflicts may arise between the youth and the shut-ins whom they visit or the substitute grandparents whom they have chosen. Role play based on the daily life or life-style of shut-ins or the elderly, or of specific conflict situations followed by discussion of the feelings of persons involved in these instances, may correct the difficulty. Also, a frank discussion of each of the difficult situations with the entire group participating may prove helpful.

For additional suggestions on coping with negative aspects of the project, see Appendix H.

HOME DEVOTIONS

In addition to the biblical passages and meditations given in the outlined sessions, the following Bible passages may be useful for home devotions: Exodus 16–24; Numbers 11–14; 20–24; John 17; Acts 4:32-37; 1 Corinthians 12:12-31; and Ephesians 4:4-13. Prayers from *The Book of Common Prayer* which are appropriate for this theme include prayers for the Second Sunday after Epiphany (page 215), for the Fifth Sunday in Lent (page 219), Propers 6, 8, and 10 (pages 230-231). For additional suggestions concerning home devotions, see Appendix I.

CELEBRATION

For general comments on using the Eucharist or Holy Communion, for the celebration, see Appendix J. In addition to the topics discussed in the outlined sessions for this unit, a service on the theme of community might point out that each one of us depends on the shared life and labors of the various members of the community (including Christ, our head) for our survival, for continuation of our physical, mental, and spiritual life. In Communion we not only receive and pledge ourselves to Christ and his life and love, but we also pledge and receive the pledges of the life and love of the other members of his body to sustain and strengthen us.

MUSIC

In addition to the hymns suggested in Session I, Step 5, in this unit, the songs "Reach Out and Touch," "Walk Together, Children," We Shall Overcome," and "Leaning on the Everlasting Arms" are appropriate for this theme.

EVALUATION

See "Suggestions for Project Evaluation," Appendix L.

Unit on Justice

Background

4

Justice is an especially important theme in the Bible. From the covenant, which establishes laws for a just society; through the prophets, who denounce Israelite society as unjust, call for the institution of justice, and look forward to the ideal reign of a just Messiah; to Jesus Christ, the longed-for Messiah who came to establish justice, biblical writings reveal a just God who is concerned to establish justice among people on earth. From these passages we get a picture that God's justice means more than treating other people fairly and being unwilling to take advantage of someone else's misfortune. We see that God's justice includes a special concern for the poor and unprotected in society. In the Bible we, in fact, see justice as the form love takes in distributing what God in love has given to all human beings so that all are cared for and can live decently. Sessions I, II, and IV in this unit help the youth explore the concept of justice as seen in the Bible.

The problem of injustice has been a major one for blacks in the United States. Because, as blacks, we continue to encounter instances of prejudice and discrimination, we need to know how to cope with these situations and the feelings they engender. Session II in this unit presents this problem. And since injustice and discrimination are crippling, blacks must continue to work toward healing the effects of past injustices. In Session III the youth can explore the history of the black church and discuss what their congregations can do presently to help heal the effects of injustice.

It is not always easy to decide what is just, as is obvious in Session I. In Session IV the youth look at the juvenile justice system as it functions in their own locale and try to balance the issues and aims found there against the biblical concepts of justice and love.

As blacks, we must continue to work for justice in the world not simply because as black people we want a better life but because God wants justice for all people on earth.

The suggested long-term projects give the youth an opportunity to work for justice in local, state, national, and international affairs.

Justice: Fair or Unfair?

PURPOSE

To enable youth

—to understand biblical concepts of justice

—to have an opportunity to wrestle with some current problems in justice and injustice

—to relate to a God whose justice is part of love

—to see justice as an important element in African traditional society

OUTLINE OF SESSION

Step 1—Ole Missy, the Mule, and the Buggy

Step 2—"To Do Justly"

Step 3—Fair and Unfair

Step 4—Prayer: The God of Justice and Love

Step 5—Justice, African Style

(Step 6—Evaluation)

Step 1—Ole Missy, the Mule, and the Buggy

Read or have someone else read or tell the following story to the group:

Old Missy was going to town to carry some eggs. So she was in a buggy driving a mule. The mule got scared and runned away and throwed Old Missy out. It didn't kill her, just bruised her up a little. So the people got the mule and buggy and drove it up to town and had the mule tried. They found the mule guilty for running away with the buggy and the buggy guilty for running away and throwing Old Missy out. So the J.P. he sentences the mule to be hung and sent the buggy to the penitentiary for life.[1]

After the story, ask the group members whether they think what happened to the mule and the buggy was fair. If so, why was it fair; if not, why not? If what happened to the mule and the buggy was not fair, why were people able to get away with it?

Comment that people who, like the mule and buggy, cannot speak up for themselves very well, who are poor, or who are not as powerful as others in the society and cannot protect themselves very well are often the victims of injustice. This was as true in biblical times as it is today.

Step 2—"To Do Justly"

Summarize the following comments as an introduction to the biblical material:

In the Bible it is the prophets who talk most about justice. Usually, when we think of prophets, we think of

[1] Reprinted from Richard M. Dorson, *American Negro Folktales* (Greenwich, Conn.: Fawcett Publications, Inc., 1967), p. 306.

someone who can tell us something about what is going to happen in the future. Although the prophets in the Bible did make some predictions about the future, this was not their main function. Their primary task was to speak as messengers from God to remind the Israelites of what God required of them as the Chosen People.

That is how many of the prophets came to talk about injustice. At the time that these prophets lived, the Israelite nobles and merchants had become very wealthy. But wealth had made them greedy, too, and injustice and oppression had become widespread. For many years these conditions continued in Israelite society.

The following verses give us an idea of what Israelite society was like at the time of the prophets and what the prophets had to say to the people.

1. Have the group read Amos 3:14-15; 6:3-7. Then ask the youth to describe how the wealthy lived. (They had summer houses and winter houses adorned with ivory, banquets with good food, etc.)

2. Have them read Isaiah 3:13-15; Jeremiah 6:13; Amos 5:11-12; 8:4-6; Micah 2:1-2; and Malachi 3:5. Explain that the gate was where the elders sat to try cases in the ancient Israelite cities. Amos is saying that the poor do not receive justice at the gate, that is, in the courts. Ask how a number of the rich got their wealth, according to these verses. (By cheating, stealing, dealing falsely and taking bribes, and by oppressing the weaker people in the society—the poor, the widow and fatherless, the hired servants, and foreigners living among them.)

3. Have the group read Amos 5:21-24; Micah 6:6-8; and Zechariah 7:8-10 to see what the prophets told the people God required of them.

4. In order for the youth to understand what was considered just and right under God's law for Israel, have the group read Leviticus 19:11, 13a, 15; Numbers 5:5-7; and Deuteronomy 24:14-15, 17-22; 25:13-16. Ask them: "What was the biblical idea of justice and righteousness then?"

5. Summarize the following comments:

For the ancient Israelites, doing what was just was not necessarily something negative—not cheating, not stealing, not dealing falsely or rendering false judgments. It was something positive as well. Justice involved making recompense to those whom one had cheated. It especially involved making sure that those who were less powerful than others in the society—the poor, the widow, the fatherless, the foreigner—were well attended. As Amos and Malachi pointed out, this was their right under Israelite law. In the Bible, justice is linked with mercy and compassion. (See Micah 6:6-11 and Zechariah 7:8-12.) It is a way of showing love and of distributing what God has given in love so that everyone in the society is cared for. It is being fair in the widest sense of the word, in the sense of seeing to it that everyone has an opportunity for a decent life in the society. The New Testament shows us that this sort of justice is what is expected of us as Christians.

6. Have the group turn to Matthew 25:31-40; Luke 3:10-11; and 2 Corinthians 8:8-15.

Step 3—Fair and Unfair

1. Comment that problems of justice, questions of what is fair and what is unfair, are still with us. They exist on all levels of human society—between two people and among groups of people and nations.

2. Divide the youth into small groups and ask each of the small groups to discuss one of the following contemporary situations and to decide, in the light of the biblical ideas concerning justice, what would be just and fair.

3. After the youth have discussed the situations, have them reassemble and ask a spokesperson from each small group to report on what was decided. Allow all to discuss the decisions.

Situation #1

Allan P. Bakke, a white American of Scandinavian extraction, a civil engineer, filed a lawsuit against the Medical School of the University of California at Davis, on the grounds that its special admission policy which reserved sixteen of the hundred first-year class places for certain racial minority students violated his rights under the equal protection clause of the Fourteenth Amendment and Title VI of the 1964 Civil Rights Act. Bakke had scored higher on objective tests for admission than any of the sixteen applicants admitted under the special admission policy, but he had not been admitted to the school. In the summer of 1978 the Supreme Court voted in favor of Bakke and ordered that he be admitted to Davis. In the decision the Supreme Court also outlawed quotas as a means of assuring members of minority groups of admission to institutions (universities, jobs, etc.) where they had previously not been admitted.

Commenting on the decision, Warner Traynham, a dean of Dartmouth College, writes:

Blacks make up roughly 12% of the nation. With respect to medicine, in 1972, the first year Mr. Bakke applied to medical school, only 1.7% of all the physicians in the country were black. With respect to health in the black community; infant mortality rate for blacks is almost double the white rate; maternal mortality is three times that of whites; and the life expectancy for blacks is substantially lower than that for whites. Now it has been shown that minority professionals tend to practice in minority areas and whites in white areas. So one could argue that the education of minority doctors is the most direct way to affect the serious health problems of minority communities.[2]

In his dissenting opinion, Supreme Court Justice Thurgood Marshall wrote:

It is of course true that some of the Jim Crow laws . . . were struck down by this Court in a series of decisions leading up to *Brown* v. *Board of Education of Topeka*. . . . Those decisions, however, did not automatically end segregation, nor did they move Negroes from a position of legal inferiority to one of equality. The legacy of years of slavery and of years of second-class citizenship in the wake of emancipation could not be so easily eliminated. The position of the Negro today in America is the tragic but inevitable consequence of centuries of unequal treatment. . . . If we are ever to become a fully integrated society, one in which the color of a person's skin will not determine the opportunities available to him or her, we must be willing to take steps to open [the doors to positions of influence, affluence, and prestige in America]. I do not believe that anyone can truly look into America's past and still find that a remedy for the effects of that past is impermissible.[3]

In view of the biblical ideas concerning justice, do you think the decision of the Supreme Court in the Bakke case was just or unjust?

Situation #2

Namibia, formerly called South West Africa, was inhabited in the nineteenth century by several African tribes. When, in the 1870s, some white South Africans passed through South West Africa on their way to Angola, the leader of one of the African tribes in the area protested and requested protection from Britain. Britain refused to withdraw, and late in the nineteenth century, Germany took over the territory. The Germans refused to allow the Africans to buy land or cattle and in wars with two of the largest African tribes killed many of them.

[2] From "Reverse Discrimination: Fact or Fiction?" Mr. Traynham's figures are taken from the brief *Amici Curiae,* Regents of the University of California v. Allan Bakke for the National Council of Churches (U.S. Supreme Court, October term, 1976), No. 76-811, pp. 11-13.

[3] Separate opinion of Mr. Justice Marshall in the syllabus of the Supreme Court of the United States. *Regents of the University of California* v. *Bakke,* pp. 8, 15.

During World War I South African troops, acting under British orders and with the help of the Africans, took over South West Africa. After the war South Africa claimed South West Africa as the spoils of war and wanted to make it part of the Union of South Africa. However, the League of Nations, formed by the victorious Allied powers after World War I, mandated Britain the trustee for South West Africa. The League also said that the mandatory power should prepare the country for independence and should not profit from administrative rights. The mandate was to be exercised on behalf of Britain by the Union of South Africa.

When at the end of World War II, the Allied powers replaced the League of Nations with the United Nations, all of the powers that had been mandated to look after territories under the League agreed that the UN Trusteeship Committee should look after the interests of the trust territories, and all brought the territories under their care to independence except South Africa. South Africa demanded that South West Africa be made a part of South Africa.

Since then, the UN General Assembly has passed a resolution ending South Africa's League of Nations mandate and making South West Africa the direct responsibility of the UN. However, South Africa held elections to elect white South West Africans to the South African House of Assembly and began to institute the same practices with regard to Africans in South West Africa as are found in South Africa. The Africans, who make up about 77 percent of the population, are allocated by tribe small pieces of practically useless land (much of South West Africa consists of desert). The whites, however, farm large tracts of good land.

In the 1950s the black South West Africans, or Namibians, began to form political parties to attempt to gain independence. SWAPO, South West African Peoples' Organization, is the largest of these parties. After South Africa had denied the UN's right to terminate their trust mandate, SWAPO formed the People's Liberation Army of Namibia and began a guerrilla war against the South African forces. Even though the International Court of Justice ordered South Africa to withdraw from Namibia and the UN Trusteeship Committee called on the Security Council to take steps to expel South Africa, the Security Council was unable to decide how to implement the decision. Thus, South Africa continued its control of South West Africa.[4]

In view of the biblical ideas concerning justice, do you think that South Africa's presence in Namibia is just or unjust?

[4] Louise Stack and Don Morton, *Torment to Triumph in Southern Africa* (New York: Friendship Press, 1976), pp. 66-77.

Situation #3

In America most taxation takes place at the state and local levels in the form of property and sales taxes and other taxes which do not take into consideration how much income a taxpayer receives. Since these taxes fall on necessary expenditures, such as food, housing, and gasoline, the poor and lower middle class pay a larger proportion of these taxes than the rich do. In 1965, those who earned less than $2,000 paid out 25 percent of what they earned in state and local taxes while those earning $15,000 or more paid only 7 percent. However, reporters in Tennessee discovered that coal-mining corporations owning thousands of acres of land in that state paid only small property taxes because their land was assessed at between $30 and $40 an acre while farmland in the same area was assessed at between $100 and $500 an acre. In Georgia, the state paid $2,000 an acre for land which it bought from a timber corporation and which, when owned by the timber company, was assessed at less than $20 an acre. In Maine, law students estimated that the state loses more than $1 million annually because timberland, belonging to corporations, is underassessed there. Yet statistics show that in 1962 the wealthiest 5 percent of the nation owned 83 percent of all the corporate stock and in 1966 for those who earned over $100,000 a year, 66.8% of their income came from capital, that is, property and investments, such as shares of stock in corporations.

In the summer of 1978 Californians passed a measure called Proposition 13, which put a ceiling on real estate taxes to be paid to the state. Under this proposal thirteen of the state's largest corporations will receive a $431.4-million tax deduction. However, since city and county governmental units and school districts depend heavily on property taxes, many services funded by these units, such as day care programs, clinics, and free trash collection, will have to be eliminated. Elimination of these services would, of course, pose a greater hardship for the poor than for the rich.

People in many other states are thinking of enacting measures similar to Proposition 13.[5]

In view of the biblical ideas concerning justice, do you think that measures such as Proposition 13 are a just or unjust way to reduce property taxes?

Situation #4

On every statistical indicator, Indians in America

[5] Campaign for Human Development, *Poverty in American Democracy* (Washington, D.C.: United States Catholic Conference, 1974), pp. 90, 99, 121, 136, 137; and Michael Emery and Suzanne Steiner Emery, "Reporting Proposition 13: Business as Usual," *Columbia Journalism Review*, November-December, 1978, pp. 31-33.

rank at the bottom. They have the highest infant mortality, the lowest life expectancy, the lowest educational level, the lowest per capita income, and the poorest transportation facilities and housing. Beginning with the Indian Removal Act of 1830, the Indians were forcibly relocated in the West, eventually forced to cede most of their lands by treaty, and were confined to reservations. Although much Indian reservation land is the land least fit for farming and grazing, some of it has recently been found to have tremendous natural resources—uranium, coal, water, and timber. Up to now the Indians have not been able to realize much profit from these resources, and presently the resources are being used and developed by non-Indian individuals and corporations.

When the Indians ceded their land to the federal government, the government took over by law certain "trust responsibilities," among which was the protection of Indian natural resources. The Bureau of Indian Affairs is the government agency charged with administering this trust. Relying on advice given by the BIA, the Crow and Northern Cheyenne Indian tribes in the 1960s signed contracts with corporations granting the corporations mining rights to the oil, gas, and coal deposits on their land. Later, they discovered that the contracts were so poor that they had nearly given away these resources. The U.S. government, however, has shown no inclination to provide money or technical assistance for the Indians to develop their resources for their own economic benefit and is, in fact, now urging Indians to leave the reservations and move to the cities.[6]

In view of the biblical ideas concerning justice, do you think the policy of the U.S. government toward the Indians has been just or unjust?

Step 4—Prayer: The God of Justice and Love

Comment that God is just and that in asking us to practice justice and to bear a special concern for the poor and powerless, we are really being asked to mirror God's justice in the world. It is this justice, a condition where all—the poor and powerless as well as the rich—receive their share of what has been given in love, that God came in Jesus Christ to initiate in the earth. Ask the group members to imagine themselves in the presence of God and to answer silently to themselves the questions which you will ask them. (The material within single quotation marks is the author's paraphrases of Scripture.)

1. "Let us begin by picturing what God is like. 'For the Lord your God is God of gods and Lord of lords, a great, mighty, and terrible God.' What picture do you get?" (Pause) "What feeling do you get?" (Pause)

2. "'He is no respecter of persons and is not to be bribed.' What picture do you get?" (Pause) "What feeling do you get?" (Pause)

3. "'He secures justice for widows and orphans, and loves the stranger who lives among you, giving him food and clothing.' What picture do you get?" (Pause) "What feeling do you get?" (Pause)

4. "'The Lord is righteous in his acts; he brings justice to all who have been wronged.' What picture do you get?" (Pause) "What feeling do you get?" (Pause)

5. "'For these are the words of the Lord God: Now I myself will ask after my sheep and go in search of them . . . I will search for the lost, recover the straggler, bandage the hurt, strengthen the sick, leave the healthy and strong to play, and give them their proper food.' What picture do you get? How do you feel about this kind of God? What sort of response would you make to this kind of God?" (Long pause)

Allow youth who wish to discuss their meditation with the group to do so.

Step 5—Justice, African Style

After giving the following background, tell the tale "The Talking Goat," teach the song, and have the members of the group act out the story. In the song the person playing the part of the goat sings the "leader" parts, and the others sing the "chorus" parts.

The ancestors of the present-day black Americans lived in West Africa. There are many different peoples living in West Africa. The Yoruba are one of those peoples. They live in the western part of Nigeria and the eastern part of the Republic of Benin. The Yoruba love to tell stories and act them out. Many of their tales are cantefables, that is, tales with songs in them.

In many Yoruba households there is more than one wife. Traditionally, Yoruba men were allowed to marry more than one woman at a time, but there may also be more than one wife in a household because married sons continue to live in the family house or compound, an area comprising several small houses. Where there is more than one wife in the household, the first wife to have married into the family is considered the head wife and directs the work of all the others.

One of the things that the wives must do is to prepare the meals for the family. The traditional Yoruba dinner usually has as its main dish a soup or stew made with meat or fish, ground onions, ground red peppers, ground tomatoes, tomato paste, cooking oil, and seasonings. Palm oil, which is a favorite oil for making

[6] Joint Strategy and Action Committee, "Grapevine," vol. 8, no. 6, January, 1977; *Hunger Notes,* Episcopal edition, vol. 4, no. 5, October, 1978; and Indian Rights Association, "American Indians Today."

soups, is thick and reddish in color, like the soup itself.

Traditionally, the Yoruba were very much concerned about justice and that everyone in the community was well taken care of. This story, "The Talking Goat," shows us something of their sense of justice.

The Talking Goat

There was once a head wife who made a good stew for dinner. She asked the second wife to warm it up. The stew smelled so good that the second wife ate it all up herself. In order to hide what she had done, she took palm oil, which is thick and reddish in color, and smeared it around a goat's mouth. Then she showed the goat to the head wife and told her that the goat had eaten the stew.

The head wife decided that any goat who eats the dinner should be killed, and so the goat was tied up outside the house until the husband came home. When the husband returned, he took the goat and was going to kill it with a machete, but it began to sing (see the song at the bottom of this page). When the husband heard the song, he let the goat go free. But he returned home and punished the second wife.

(Step 6—Evaluation)

To evaluate the session with members of the group, see the suggestions given in Appendix E.

[1] "Me" is pronounced "maa," rhyming with "baa." It is how the Yoruba imitate the sound a sheep or goat makes.

A Program on Justice

PURPOSE

To enable youth

—to experience how it feels to be the victims of prejudice and discrimination

—to explore ways for coping with both prejudice and discrimination and the feelings these experiences bring into being

OUTLINE OF SESSION

Step 1—Setting Up the Program
Step 2—"The Way of Justice Is Uprightness"
Step 3—A Program of Justice, Part I
Step 4—Ricky
Step 5—A Program of Justice, Part II
Step 6—Prayer: "Come, Lord, Save and Heal"
(Step 7—Evaluation)

Step 1—Setting Up the Program

1. Place a pile of newspapers and newsmagazines and several pairs of scissors neatly on a large table. On a small, dirty table, already littered with other things, place one newsmagazine and a pair of scissors.

2. As the members of the group arrive, use some method to assign persons to sit at one table or the other. You can, for example, decide that every other person sits at the small table, or you can use different colored tokens to decide who sits where.

Step 2—"The Way of Justice Is Uprightness"

Tell the group that in this session they will outline a presentation on justice. Give a summary of the biblical background on justice found in Step 2 of "Justice: Fair or Unfair," Session I. While giving the summary, keep your back turned to the group at the small, littered table, and ignore any comments and questions they may try to make. However, encourage questions and comments from the group at the large table.

Step 3—A Program of Justice, Part I

1. Ask the youth to cut out of the newspapers and magazines articles dealing with justice and injustice. These may include accounts of trials, nonsexist want ads, articles on the countries of southern Africa, D.C. voting rights, the Equal Rights Amendment, welfare and health services reform, etc. Tell the group that they may use only the materials found on the table where they are seated.

2. Ask each of the two groups, when they have finished cutting out articles, to prepare an outline for a presentation on justice based on the information they have found and the biblical background concerning justice which they heard (Step 2, Session I).

3. Have each group choose a spokesperson who will present the outline prepared by the group.

4. Allow fifteen or twenty minutes for this exercise and then ask the spokesperson to read the outlines.

5. No matter how well either outline was prepared, when the spokespersons are finished, praise the group at the large table while ignoring the other group.

6. Ask everyone whether or not they think the group at the small table has been treated fairly and justly during the session. Ask the group members at the small table how they feel about themselves, about the group at the large table, and about the entire situation as a result of the way they have been treated.

7. Comment that the next part of the session will explore ways of dealing with situations of prejudice and discrimination and the feelings these situations bring about.

Step 4—Ricky

1. Read or tell to the group the story of Ricky (see below) and the different possible endings which are provided for the story.

2. Ask the members of the group to indicate which ending they would choose and why they prefer that ending.

Then, continue with the discussion questions.

Ricky

Ricky was Puerto Rican. He always studied hard at school and obeyed all the school rules so that his family would be proud of him.

One day, Ricky's history teacher told the class that there would be a test the next day. She said that she would give them time to study that afternoon and then assigned groups of four to work together. Ricky was unhappy when the teacher called the names of the other people in his group. The other three boys were black, and they did not like Ricky because he was Puerto Rican. When Ricky came over to study, they made a game of keeping the book away from him.

"Get away. We don't want to work with any Puerto Ricans," they continued to mutter under their breath.

Ricky didn't know what to do. Should he tell his teacher that the boys wouldn't let him work with them because he was Puerto Rican? What those boys were doing was wrong, and Ricky knew that. But if he told the teacher, things could get worse. The boys might get angry and hurt him. Things would surely be safer for Ricky if he kept quiet and studied on his own.

Here are five different possible endings for Ricky's story. Which do you think he should choose?

1. Ricky decided to tell the teacher. The teacher told the boys that they would either have to let Ricky study with them or she would have the principal suspend them.

2. Ricky looked straight at the boys. He told them that what they were doing was wrong, that he was very angry, and that since the teacher had told him to sit where he was, he was not going to move.

3. Ricky got angrier by the minute. He whispered to the boys that he would fight them all after school.

4. After school Ricky rushed home. He sat down across from his mother and told her what had happened. Then his mother said, "I know you feel bad about it, but you mustn't let it get you down. You're as good as anybody else, and don't you ever let anyone tell you you're not."

5. Ricky moved a little away from the boys. They kept on laughing and saying rude things about him under their breath. But Ricky didn't hear them. He was busy studying. When he got home, Ricky began to study some more. He was determined to do well and show those boys. The next day Ricky got all the answers right on the test, and all of the other boys flunked.

Discussion Questions

1. "Do you think that any of those things that Ricky could do would keep the boys from ever being prejudiced against him again?" (No.)

2. "How do you think Ricky felt when the boys refused to work with him and began to say things about him because he was Puerto Rican?" (Angry? Sad? Ashamed that he was Puerto Rican?)

3. "Was it right for Ricky to feel angry because of what happened to him?" (Yes. The boys had done something mean to him and had hurt him even though he had done nothing to them. It would be natural for Ricky to be angry. But even though he was angry, Ricky could still choose whether he would express his anger by fighting, or, perhaps, by telling the boys that he was angry, or whether he would not express it.)

4. "Was it right for Ricky to feel sad?" (Yes. We often feel sad when people refuse to have anything to do with us.)

5. "Was it right for Ricky to feel ashamed that he was Puerto Rican?" (We often do feel ashamed when people are prejudiced against us or call us names because we are black or Puerto Rican or anything else.

Being black or Puerto Rican or anything else is nothing to be ashamed of, though. God made us whatever we are.)

6. "Which of the endings to the story do you think made Ricky feel better? Which would have made you feel better?"

7. "Do you think that you could always do whatever happened in the ending which you chose whenever you had to face prejudice and discrimination?" (You cannot always do the same thing when you are faced by prejudice and discrimination. What is best to do in any situation often depends on the situation.)

Step 5—A Program of Justice, Part II

1. Have the group read Acts 10:9-28 and Genesis 1:31.

2. Comment that in the first-century Jews felt that all other peoples were inferior to them because God had not given the law to these other peoples. Because of this, Jews would not eat or associate with non-Jews. However, God showed Peter that he should think of no one as inferior. It is God who made peoples differ one from the other, and everything that God made is good.

3. Ask all the youth to join together to create a revised outline for their presentation on justice. Have them include what they have learned concerning prejudice and discrimination in the outline. Decide on a date when they can make their presentation before an audience, on who will do which parts, etc.

Step 6—Prayer: "Come, Lord, Save and Heal"

1. Have the youth picture themselves in the presence of Christ. (Pause)

2. Have them recall some occasion in their personal lives when they have encountered prejudice and discrimination. (If they have never personally experienced prejudice and discrimination, ask them to act as a "stand-in" for someone who has.) (Pause)

3. Ask them to try to experience again how they felt at that time, or how the person who was the victim of prejudice and discrimination felt if they have never had a personal experience. (Pause)

4. Have them imagine what the feeling looked like. Did it look like a hot, swollen-faced person because they were so angry or ashamed? Did it have tears in its eyes because they were hurt or sad? (Pause)

5. Have the youth give this image to Christ and ask him to heal it. (Pause)

(Step 7—Evaluation)

To evaluate the session with the group, see the suggestions given in Appendix E.

Injustice Is Crippling; Healing the Cripple

PURPOSE

To enable youth
- —to see how injustice is crippling
- —to see how the Body of Christ can go about healing the crippling effects of past injustices

OUTLINE OF SESSION

Step 1—"Bent Double"
Step 2—Our Legacy from the Past
Step 3—Healing the Cripple
Step 4—Prayer: "Know the Healing Power of His Love"
Step 5—Activity: "I Danced in the Morning"
(Step 6—Evaluation)

Step 1—"Bent Double"

1. Read, or have someone read, Luke 13:10-13.
2. Have the group divide into small groups of two.
3. Have the groups of two role-play the Scripture as it is read again. The first time the role play is done, have one of the duo take the part of the woman and the other the part of Jesus.
4. Repeat the role play, but the second time have those who played the woman be Jesus and those who played Jesus be the woman. Then use the following questions for discussion.
5. "As the woman, what were you able to see when you were bent over? What were you able to do? How did you feel about yourself? How did you feel about other people? How did you think other people felt about you?"
6. "What could you see when you straightened up? What could you do? How did you feel about yourself? How did you feel about other people? How did you think other people felt about you?"
7. "As Jesus, how did you feel when you saw the woman bent over? When you touched her? When she was healed? When she began to praise God?"

After these questions have been answered, summarize these comments: There are many ways that people may be crippled or deformed or bent over. For example, we speak of people being crippled because they didn't have much schooling. Injustice is another thing that tends to cripple people. And just as Jesus Christ healed and freed from their disabilities those who were crippled and enabled them to lead fuller lives, the church, which is the Body of Christ in the world (1 Corinthians 12:12-13, 27; Colossians 1:18a, 24), must act to heal and free those who have been crippled by injustice and thus enable them to realize their full human potential.

Step 2—Our Legacy from the Past

Continue with a summary of the following: Throughout its history the black church has attempted to provide for its people healing from the crippling effects of the injustice and discrimination which they suffered in the general society. In fact, the first black denomination and the first black Episcopal congregation in the United States were founded as a response to the discrimination which black Christians had to face in the church.

Shortly after the American Revolution, as the number of free black Christians began to grow, white churches in the North attempted to force their black members to accept segregated seating in the balcony or back pews of the church buildings. When, in Saint George's Methodist Church in Philadelphia, the trustees decreed that all blacks should sit in the balcony, Richard Allen and Absalom Jones and a large body of black believers left the church to form the Free African Society. The Free African Society provided funds for sickness and burial and cared for widows and dependent children, functions which were continued when, from the Free African Society, Allen formed Bethel African Methodist Episcopal Church and Absalom Jones founded Saint Thomas African Episcopal Church. Bethel, the mother church of the A.M.E. denomination, also became a "station" for fugitive slaves traveling along the Underground Railroad. Both Allen and Jones were active in the fight to abolish slavery and supported many schemes to undermine the institution.

Slavery, oppression, and discrimination threatened to cripple blacks by robbing them of their sense of dignity and worth as human beings, but black preachers like Jones and Allen, using Psalm 68:31 as a text, proclaimed that black Americans were a chosen people, brought to America by God to pursue a great task. For some, this task was in behalf of all humanity; for others, it was essentially confined to Christianizing Africa.

In the nineteenth century many black American Christians went as missionaries to Africa. Perhaps one of the best known was the Reverend Lott Carey, a Baptist from Virginia, who organized the African

Missionary Society and who sailed to Liberia with some of the Americans who emigrated there. Although the earliest Afro-American missionaries were primarily concerned with "preaching the Gospel to the heathen," later black American missionaries, such as Alexander Crummell, an Episcopalian, came to appreciate the value and beauty of traditional African culture and returned to encourage their people in the fight for black dignity and self-respect.

After the Civil War the black church and its people played a major role in providing the services so desperately needed by blacks at that time. By law the slaves had been denied schooling and education. Many of the new schools opened for the newly freed slaves were under church auspices. By 1900, for example, there were approximately one hundred Episcopal Church schools for blacks in the South. As blacks from the rural South began to move to the North, it was the black church that provided them with a sense of community, helped them make a rapid adjustment to urban living, and was a constant source of help. Many large black churches in northern cities, such as Abyssinian Baptist Church and Saint Phillip's Episcopal Church in New York City, became known for their involvement in housing, recreation, politics, and other social welfare areas. Black church ministers were not only able preachers but, in striving to care for the total needs of their people, became skilled in social work and political organization as well.

Where blacks were part of predominantly white denominations, as, for example, in the case of the black Presbyterians and Episcopalians, the educational standards for ordination of the denomination often hampered the growth of black congregations, since there were few black clergy available in these denominations and many whites were unwilling to minister to blacks. However, the black denominations, the black Baptists and Methodists, became a fertile training ground for both clergy and lay leadership. Blacks who suffered humiliation, degradation, and a sense of being "nobody" in their daily lives, at church were given an opportunity to develop not only a sense of personhood and self-confidence but skills in organization, decision making, planning, and public speaking as well.

Although the black church involvement in protest and struggle against injustice seemed to lay dormant for a time, it was to break forth again under the Reverend Dr. Martin Luther King, Jr., in the civil rights movement of the 1960s which was organized in and led by the black churches in the South. But although the civil rights movement brought some social advances for blacks, mainly through integrating many public facilities, some black church people saw that black people could not be truly free or receive their just due as long as the white economic and political power structure of the nation continued to control their destiny by controlling the means of production and employment and thus where blacks could afford to live, send their children to school, receive health care, etc. These persons, and most notably the Reverend Dr. James Cone, saw blacks, despite the social gains of the sixties, as still essentially an oppressed people, and they enunciated a black theology of liberation.

Black liberation theology, which is current today, actually includes many of the themes which have been part of the theology of black people in America for a long time. Absalom Jones, in the eighteenth century, said that God "acted in history in behalf of oppressed nations" as "deliverer of the innocent," and Cone says that, too. Black theology also embraces the themes of protest and chosenness, also seen before in the history of the black church. This theology sees God especially at work in and with those who are oppressed in order to free them from poverty and injustice and all else that would deny or distort their humanity. Thus, in protesting against injustice and oppression, the black church continues to try to heal the crippling which injustice causes.

Step 3—Healing the Cripple

1. Divide the youth into small groups.

2. Assign each group one of the situations below. Ask them (a) to determine how and what happened in the situation which might prove to be crippling and (b) to determine how, judging from the history of the black church, the church today might go about healing the wounds that have resulted from the experience.

3. Have a spokesperson from each group describe for the entire body the situation discussed in his or her group and what the group decided.

4. After all the situations have been discussed, you may wish to have the entire group outline how the youth or the congregation might actually begin work to heal people who are crippled in these ways in your community.

Situation #1

Joereen had moved with her five children far away from the small Southern rural community where she had been born. She had come North to the city because her cousin had told her that she was sure she could get a job easily. Now that she was here, Joereen discovered that all the jobs that were available required some sort of special training, and she hadn't even finished eighth grade. She was, in fact, lucky to have gotten that much schooling since every time she got started, she'd had to stop and help out with the crop. She wasn't really sorry

64

because her family could never have made it if all the kids hadn't come out of school to help with the crop. But now she couldn't get a job, and she couldn't stay with her cousin anymore because it was too crowded. She had no money for food, and her kids were crying because they were hungry. What's more, she didn't know anybody in this city except her cousin. The people at the welfare office said that she couldn't get help until she had lived in that city longer. But she had no money to live on now.

How has Joereen been crippled in this situation? Judging from the history of the black church, how do you think your congregation might act to heal that crippling?

Situation #2

Granny had saved some money so that Derek could go to Winston, a private high school, just like the rich white boys do. She said that the schools in the ghetto, where Derek lived, were no good and that Derek needed to go to a good high school so that he could go to a good college and get a good job. Derek worked hard and was able to keep up in the classes, but he never could get to do the thing he wanted most to do. He wanted to act in some of the plays around the school; but every time he tried out, the drama teacher turned him down. She said that at good schools like Winston they only put on Shakespeare and other classics and that Derek's black Southern accent wouldn't sound right in the classics. Besides, the drama teacher had continued, Derek really didn't know how to speak in front of people.

How is Derek being crippled in this situation? Judging from the history of the black church, how do you think your congregation might act to heal that crippling?

Situation #3

Doreetha sat across from the admissions clerk at the hospital. She still couldn't believe what she had just heard. The doctor had told her that her two-year-old daughter, Leeta, had sickle-cell anemia and had to be hospitalized. He had also told her that people with sickle-cell anemia usually don't live very long.

"Are you on welfare?" the admissions clerk asked. In fact, he had shouted the question so loudly that everyone in the room must have heard him.

"Yes," whispered Doreetha.

"What did you say?" asked the admissions clerk. "Honestly, someone ought to teach these people to stop mumbling and to speak up. Now, are you on welfare or not?"

"I'm on welfare," Doreetha answered a little more loudly.

"Well, take this form and fill it out," said the admissions clerk. "Then bring it back to me."

Doreetha looked at the form. The questions were hard, and she didn't know the answers. She wished there was someone there who could help her, but she was all alone.

How has Doreetha been crippled in this situation? From the history of the black church, how do you think your congregation might act to heal that crippling?

Situation #4

Fish and Monk had laughed until they were out of breath. They were talking about the new boy in class. When he had first come, Mr. Jones, the teacher, had said that his name was Yinka and that he was from Africa. Fish had yelled out, "Hey, Mr. Jones, you got it wrong! His name ain't 'Yinka'; it's 'Kinka' for all those kinks on his head." And they'd all had a good laugh right there.

But that was only the beginning. You could get a laugh a day out of that boy. He was always walking around acting like he owned everything and trying to talk so proper. And, lie! That boy could lie like anything! Monk had asked him if he'd ever killed a tiger with a spear, and he'd said that there aren't any tigers in Africa. Wonder when Yinka, or Kinka, or whatever his name was was ever going to stop trying to be so smart and realize that, as ugly and black as he was, he might as well just act like other people do?

How have Fish and Monk been crippled? Judging from the history of the black church, how do you think your congregation might act to heal that crippling?

Step 4—Prayer: "Know the Healing Power of His Love"

1. Have the youth imagine that they are in the presence of Christ. (Pause)

2. Have the members of the group think of someone (themselves or another person) who has been crippled by injustice. (Pause)

3. Have them picture to themselves how this person has been crippled. (Pause)

4. Have them imagine that they have brought this person to Christ. Have them ask him to heal the person. (Pause)

5. Ask the members of the group to see the person as healed and what he or she is able to do after being cured. (Pause)

6. Have them thank God for the healing. (Pause)

Allow those who wish to discuss their meditation with the group to do so.

Step 5—Activity: "I Danced in the Morning"

1. Ask the members of the group to consider which

of the crippling situations discussed during the session and its healing might be acted out in dance or mime.

2. Have the youth create a dance or mime to the music of "I Danced in the Morning" (H-63 in *More Hymns and Spiritual Songs* [Walton Music Corporation], 1977) or some other appropriate music.

(Step 6—Evaluation)

To evaluate the session with the group, see the suggestions given in Appendix E.

A Panel on Juvenile Justice

PURPOSE

To enable youth
— to gain some knowledge of the aims, workings, etc., of the juvenile justice system
— to understand the concept of justice as shown in the Bible
— to explore some specific questions concerning juvenile justice

OUTLINE OF SESSION

PART A (before the event)
Step 1—Justice in the Bible
Step 2—Justice for Juveniles, 20th century, U.S.A.
Step 3—We Invite You
Step 4—Prayer

PART B (the event)
1. Panel discussion
2. Questions from the floor
3. Closing intercessions given freely from the floor for the persons, events, and questions of concern that were discussed.

The proposed panel discussion on juvenile justice involves a two-part outline. The first part, a preparation for the actual panel discussion, takes place at a regular session with the group. Before this meeting, however, those who will lead the session should do some prior research on aspects of the juvenile justice system which they think will be of interest to the group (some suggested topics are given below). There should be as many leaders and topics chosen as the number of small groups you intend to have in PART A, Step 2, below. The leaders can be either youth or adults. Ask each of the leaders to research one of the topics below or some other topic concerning juvenile justice which would be of interest to your group. Have available, also, the names of several persons involved in the juvenile justice system in your community who might be willing to serve on the panel; possible dates and places where the panel discussion can be held; and, if you wish to use stencils or potato prints to make invitations (PART A, Step 3), the necessary materials for that.

Here are some suggested topics on juvenile justice:
• The workings of the juvenile justice system. What sorts of matters are brought to juvenile court? What are the aims of the juvenile justice system? What are the procedures used there?

• The rights of juveniles. Many have argued that our present juvenile justice system does not adequately protect the rights of juveniles because, among other reasons, it does not generally provide juvenile offenders with representation by legal counsel. Does this seem to be true?

• Can the present juvenile justice system really carry out the dual task of protecting the community from juveniles who threaten life and property and of training and reforming youthful offenders? Is there any proof that the juvenile justice system is or is not doing this task well in your community?

• Should violent juveniles be tried as adults? What are the advantages and disadvantages for the juvenile and for the community?

• Does race or social class seem to play any part in who is brought as an offender before juvenile court in your community or how the case is decided? If race or social class does seem to be a factor, what proof is there of such a claim?

PART A: Step 1—Justice in the Bible

Give the summary of the biblical material concerning justice found in "Justice: Fair or Unfair," Session I, Step 2.

PART A: Step 2—Justice for Juveniles, 20th century, U.S.A.

1. Divide the group into small groups. Provide each group with a leader who has already researched a topic relating to juvenile justice. Ask each group to appoint a recorder who will report on the topic and the group discussion when the entire body reassembles.

2. Have each leader summarize the topic for his or her group.

3. Ask each group to discuss how the biblical notions of justice relate to the topic. Also, ask the members of each group to decide whether or not they would like to obtain more information concerning the topic from a panel of professionals in the juvenile justice system.

4. Have all the youth reassemble. Ask each recorder to give a report of what happened in his or her group.

5. From the entire group draw up a list of the topics which they would like a panel of professionals to discuss.

6. Make suggestions as to who should be on the panel. (Local judges, probation officers, chaplains, etc., might be willing to participate.) Suggest, or ask

the youth to suggest names of persons who might serve as moderator. Suggest possible dates, places, and times for the panel discussion.

7. Assign persons to contact the possible panelists and to inform them of the topics the group particularly wants discussed.

If you wish, have the youth decide on an outline for the panel discussion. One possible outline is given in Part B of the session outline above.

PART A: Step 3—We Invite You

Have the members of the group design or pick symbols which they think are appropriate for the topic of juvenile justice, and then potato-print, stencil, or draw invitations for the panelists and for those who they would especially like to invite to the panel discussion. The group can also make posters to advertise the event.

PART A: Step 4—Prayer

Close with an appropriate prayer, perhaps from *The Book of Common Prayer,* such as no. 21, "For Courts of Justice," p. 821, or no. 37, "For Prisons and Correctional Institutions," p. 826 (with the terms "jails and prisons" and "prisoners" changed to reflect the juvenile justice system), or some other appropriate prayer.

PART B (the event)

Hold the panel discussion on the date decided upon, allowing for questions from the youth. For the closing, either use the prayers suggested in PART A, Step 4 or have free intercession from the youth about concerns raised by the panel discussion. You may want to evaluate the panel discussion directly after the event or during the next youth meeting. (See the suggestions given in Appendix E.)

Unit on Values and Identity

——Background——

5

Value choices and rankings express who we are individually. The things that we value and the order in which we rank those things may vary greatly from person to person, from one culture to another, and from one religious system to another. Session I in this unit is designed to help youth develop an appreciation and respect for themselves, for one another, and for individual differences as expressed in value choices and ranking.

Conflict over value choices and rankings is a frequent cause of tension within persons and between and among persons in society. Session II in this unit discusses the struggle between Israelite and Canaanite religions, which is described in the Old Testament, as a value conflict. In this value conflict the Israelite worship of Yahweh stressed values of compassion, respect, and concern for all in the community, while the Canaanite Baal worship tended to stress the importance of material increase. Since this basic conflict is found also in American society, the session attempts to reinforce the human relational values of Israelite religion as being important for contemporary black Christians, too.

There are many factors which influence our value choices. Session III is designed to enable the youth to look critically at these factors so that they will be able to strain out those influences which would destroy who they are or who they want to be.

Value Ranking

PURPOSE

To enable youth
—to look at different values which were important to their racial and spiritual ancestors
—to discover which values are of greatest importance to them
—to discuss how they might go about acting on their most important values
—to make some commitment to act on their most important values

OUTLINE OF SESSION

Step 1—Onisara
Step 2—What Would You Die For?
Step 3—How Can You Live for It?
Step 4—Prayer: Commitment
(Step 5—Evaluation)

Step 1—Onisara

As a prelude to looking at what is of great importance to them, the group members will look at some of the values of their racial and spiritual ancestors. In the song "Onisara"[1] they will see some of the values of the Yoruba of Nigeria.

The ancestors of the present-day black Americans came from West Africa, where the Yoruba live. Among the Yoruba, when a child recovers from a serious illness, she or he is often treated to a *sara,* a traditional feast. Other children are invited to the *sara,* and together with *onisara,* the one who has the *sara,* they eat and sing and dance. They may also play *ayo,*[2] a complex African game played with seeds.

Have the members of your group form a circle and dance single file clockwise around the circle in time with the music as the song is sung. After the dance, ask, "According to the song, what are the things that are important to the Yoruba people? What do they value? Are these things which many of the people you know value?" The song is on page 72.

Step 2—What Would You Die For?

Read or have someone read the following two sketches ("Joshua" and "Toussaint L'Ouverture").

Joshua

After the Israelites were freed from slavery in Egypt, Moses led them through the wilderness toward

[1] Onisara—pronounced "Oh-knee-sah-rah."
[2] Ayo—pronounced "Eye-yo."

Canaan, the Promised Land. Moses died in the wilderness, but he commissioned his aide, Joshua, to take the people into the land of Canaan, which was already settled by numerous tribes. The Israelites knew that they would have to fight the Canaanites in order to secure a homeland in Canaan, and many of the people did not believe that they could win. However, the Israelites also believed that God wanted them to live in freedom in the Promised Land, free to direct their own destiny and to serve God as they pleased. Thus, they crossed the Jordan River into Canaan behind the ark of the covenant, the symbol of God in their midst. After they had laid siege at the city of Jericho, which seemed to them to fall by an act of God, the Israelites continued over a period of years with the conquest of Canaan.

Toussaint L'Ouverture

Toussaint was born a black slave on an island called Saint Domingue in the eighteenth century. Half of Saint Domingue was owned by the French, and half was owned by the Spanish. In 1789, revolution broke out in France, and the French revolutionaries declared that they were fighting for the freedom, brotherhood, and equality of all people. The slaves in Saint Domingue felt that they should have their freedom, too. Toussaint organized them to fight against the French masters and won so many victories that he was called "L'Ouverture," which means "the opening." Finally, in 1793, the French National Assembly proclaimed the slaves free. However, when Napoleon became emperor of France, he tried to reenslave the blacks in Saint Domingue. Toussaint was captured and died in prison, but his forces defeated the French, declared their part of the island a republic, and called it Haiti.

After the two selections have been read, ask the group:

1. "What seemed to be most important for the Israelites under Joshua?" (Obtaining freedom and following what they felt to be the will of God.)

2. "What seemed most important for Toussaint and the slaves in Saint Domingue?" (Freedom.)

Comment that we can often tell what is important to people, what they value, by seeing what they decide to do. Some people value some things so much that they are willing to die for them.

3. Have the group read John 10:11-18 and Romans 5:6-11.

4. Ask: "According to these verses, for what was Jesus Christ willing to lay down his life?" (For the benefit of those whom he, as Shepherd, led; to fulfill the divine command, to reconcile us to God.)

5. Comment that different people value different things highly. Then have each member of the group name the three things, people, etc., which are most important to him or her.

6. Ask the youth if they would be willing to die for any of these. Is there anything for which they would be willing to die?

Step 3—How Can You Live for It?

1. Give each member of the group a piece of paper and pencil.

2. Ask them to write on the paper the three things which they said were most important to them.

3. Comment that the things we say we value most are not really valuable to us unless we are willing to act on them, to do something about them.

4. Ask the youth to circle on their papers the one item that is of greatest importance to them and then figure out approximately how much time and money they spend on this item each week.

5. Ask the members of the group if it seems, from the amount of time and/or money they spend on the item they circled on their sheets, that it is really that important to them.

6. If they spend only a little time and/or money on the thing they designated as most important to them, ask the members of the group to think of ways, within the limitations set by their parents, schoolwork, etc., to spend more time or money on what they value most. Could they sacrifice some time spent watching television to work on it? Save money by giving up after school snacks? Have them write down the ways which come to mind.

Step 4—Prayer: Commitment

1. Ask those who would like to make a commitment to God to act more positively on the things they say they value to place their papers in a pile in the center of the group.

2. Ask those who wish to make the commitment to imagine themselves in the presence of Christ, to make the commitment to him, and to ask his help in acting on their values.

(Step 5—Evaluation)

To evaluate the session with the group, see the suggestions given in Appendix E.

Onisara

Value Conflict

PURPOSE

To enable youth
—to discover some of their own personal values
—to examine instances of value conflict
—to see the struggle between Israelite and Canaanite religions as a value conflict
—to see respect, compassion, and concern for all in community as important values for our life together today

OUTLINE OF SESSION

Step 1—"Dignity": A Simulation Game
Step 2—Discussing "Dignity"
Step 3—Israelites and Canaanites
Step 4—Prayer: Rethinking Old Choices
(Step 5—Evaluation)

This session involves a simulation game, "Dignity," which can be purchased for $6.95 from your local Christian bookstore.

Before the session, familiarize yourself thoroughly with the game, with the additional cards for playing the game given in Appendix D, and with the discussion and evaluation questions in Step 2 below. Cut out the additional cards and have them and the rest of the game ready to play. You may want to paste the page to a piece of cardboard and then cut the cards out so that they will be easier to handle.

Step 1—"Dignity": A Simulation Game

Play the game "Dignity" according to the rules included with the game. Limit play to forty-five minutes or an hour, and then begin the discussion in Step 2.

Step 2—Discussing "Dignity"

Use the following questions for discussion and evaluation of the game experience:

1. "How did you feel about 'the system' when you had to go back? About the other players (or teams)? About yourself? Do you think in real life these feelings would help or hinder you?"

2. "How did you feel about the other players (or the other teams) when their decisions forced you to go back?"

3. "How did you feel when your decisions forced another player (or team) to go back?"

4. "How did you feel when you got stuck in the shantytown or public housing locations on the board?"

5. "How did you feel about 'the system' when you were able to move ahead without any problem? About the other players (or teams)? About yourself? Do you think these feelings in real life might help or hinder you?"

6. "Who among the players did the group perceive as 'good guys'? Who were the 'bad guys'? Who were in between?"

7. "Did you make action choices in the context of the game that you wouldn't think of making in real life? Why did you make these choices in the game?"

8. "Were there any cards that you played with which you disagreed? What would you rather have done?"

9. "What is dignity in contemporary life? What is dignity in your religion?"

Step 3—Israelites and Canaanites

Summarize the following comments for the group: Just as in the game we've played, there are many times in life when we find ourselves in value-conflict situations. Sometimes it is because the values that we hold conflict with those of the other people around us. In other cases, it is because we ourselves act in a way which is contrary to values we think are important. Whatever may be the case, value conflict itself is not new.

When the ancient Israelites entered Canaan, the Promised Land, they had already made a covenant, or agreement, with God to lead a life according to certain values. Unfortunately, those values were often in conflict with the values held by the people already living in Canaan, the Canaanites.

By the time the Israelites settled in Canaan, the Canaanites had already established their own life-style. They lived in well-built houses and had a society made up of various classes: rich landowners, a king, and a subject population of farmers and slaves. Canaanite society was concerned with agriculture and commerce, and the people worshiped as gods Baal and his consorts, whom they thought would guarantee the fertility of their farms and the success of their businesses. In this society material success and money-making were more valued than a concern for the well-being of everyone in the society and peaceful relationships among people. And Canaanite religion, or what we know of it today, seemed to teach that human beings could, to some extent, control the gods and, through them, the forces of nature which have a bearing on agricultural success.

The religion which the Israelites held when they entered Canaan, on the other hand, was quite different. Yahweh, the God whom the Israelites worshiped, the God whom we worship, could be controlled by no one. It was out of Yahweh's own kindness and goodness that Yahweh had shown concern for the Israelites, had delivered them from slavery in Egypt, had provided for them in the desert, and had led them to Canaan, the Promised Land (Deuteronomy 7:7-8). In compassion, justice, and mercy God was concerned that the people have all the material things necessary to sustain life, but God also willed that the Israelites should be like God and live with justice, compassion, and mercy for one another. It was this concern for justice, peace, and love in society which was most important in Israelite religion. In the covenant which the Israelites had made with God they had promised to allow God's will to rule their community. By communing with God and by loving God above all else, the Israelites hoped to be able to keep the rules of the covenant, to allow God's will to work through them, and thus to bring into being a just, peaceful, loving society where each person was concerned for the well-being of everyone else in the community.

When the Israelites moved into Canaan, it was natural that they would be interested in Canaanite life. They borrowed many good things from their neighbors—agricultural methods, rituals, and celebrations which, when adapted, enabled the Israelites to improve their knowledge and worship of their own God. But many Israelites also began to accept as most important the things the Canaanites valued most. They began to value material success above everything else. Since it is impossible to be concerned both with gaining greater material success for oneself and securing the well-being of all the people in the society, a value conflict occurred. Some Israelites began to amass riches and to forget about their poor brothers and sisters. They, in fact, began to act unjustly against the poorer and weaker members of the community in order to obtain greater wealth (see, e.g., Amos 2:6-7; 8:4-6; and Jeremiah 6:13). The Israelite prophets, true servants of the Israelite God, Yahweh, denounced what was going on and declared that the influence of the Canaanite religion and worship of Baal had caused the Israelites to forget their covenant with Yahweh and the values of respect, compassion, and concern for all which it stressed.

As the Israelites were influenced by the Canaanite society, so blacks in the U.S. have been greatly influenced by the overall values of American society. Although traditional African societies stressed a concern for all in the community, the slaves who were brought to this country, and later free blacks, were constantly encouraged to change and conform to the values stressed here. Blacks were taught that black or African culture is inferior to white culture. Of course, we now know that that is not true. But the belief in black inferiority, which was used to justify slavery and the system of legal segregation, brought about great pressure to conform to the ways of the white society.

To survive in America, it was, of course, necessary for blacks to learn much from the general society. Reading, writing, and speaking English were essential tools. Also, it has become increasingly important for blacks to learn to live in a technical society. But there was danger in accepting all the values of this society.

Americans have always placed great importance on money-making as a measure of success. American society tends to see money as an indication that one has worked hard. Other factors which inhibit money-making—such as an inadequate education; the effects of long-term, widespread discrimination; a low inherited status; and lack of social connections—are often ignored, and lack of concern for the less fortunate is excused on the grounds that the poor are poor solely because they haven't worked hard enough.

It is, of course, necessary for all of us to work to obtain money to purchase the necessities of life. God, who provided for the ancient Israelites in the desert, wills that we have food, warm clothing, and healthful homes, all of which are normally obtained by working. These things are necessary for the well-being of all and peace in the community.

But we cannot have peace and justice and well-being for all in the community if we come to worship money-making and material success and allow them to rule us. Many in America, as in Canaan, are controlled by these false gods. But too great a concern for money-making and material success conflicts with the ability to accord respect and demonstrate compassion and concern for all in the society. It is impossible to get rich and stay rich if you are so compassionate and concerned for the poor that you are willing to share equally with others what you have. Neither will there be true justice in a society where making money is more important to everyone than what happens to other people. And when justice, respect, compassion, and concern for all are lacking in society, there can be no peace because those who suffer injustices and who are poor, while others are rich, are tempted to turn to violence to get what others have.

Throughout the history of this nation, we as black people have suffered because an overriding concern for material success in this society has deprived us of justice, dignity, and respect. Although this was most obvious during slavery when our ancestors were forced to work to make someone else rich, it is still true today.

The desire to make profit, to amass and protect material gain, still dominates the decisions and priorities set in this country. Recent hearings held by the Urban Bishops Coalition in the Episcopal Church found that outright discrimination still prevents some qualified blacks from competing for jobs, for example, in the building and construction industry. They found, also, that poor people in our inner cities, many of whom are black, are being forced out of their dwellings as the cities are rebuilt with housing that these people cannot afford.

If we would be the people of God, then we cannot allow a desire to make money outweigh our concern for justice and for the well-being of the poor in our society, many of whom are our own black sisters and brothers. We must maintain communion with the compassionate, merciful, and just God whom we worship so that God's Spirit working in, through, and with us will enable us to act with compassionate concern, and work toward the loving, just, and peaceful society which God wills.

Step 4—Prayer: Rethinking Old Choices

Comment that the values of respect, compassion, and concern for others can conflict with other values in addition to those centered on money-making. Our desire to prove our own worth can, for example, cause us to act without concern for the dignity and rights of others.

1. Have the members of the group imagine that they are in the presence of Christ. (Pause)

2. Have them recall a situation where their desire for greater personal gain, of whatever kind, has caused them to act without compassion and concern. (Pause)

3. Have the youth bring this situation and the person or persons involved to Christ. (Pause)

4. Have them ask Christ to forgive them, to show them what they should have done, and to give them the will to do it in the future. (Pause)

(Step 5—Evaluation)

To evaluate the session with the group, see the suggestions given in Appendix E.

Session III

What Influences Our Values?

PURPOSE

To enable youth
—to discover some of the things they like or dislike
—to identify some of the factors which influence their value choices
—to look critically at value choices

OUTLINE OF SESSION

Step 1—Shopping Trip
Step 2—Discussing the Shopping Trip
Step 3—Does It Fit?
Step 4—Activity: Part of Me
Step 5—Prayer: Being Me
(Step 6—Evaluation)

Before the session, collect empty containers, cut out advertisements, and make facsimile labels to represent popular foods and music (or other areas of life if you wish) from many different cultures and peoples. (You may, for example, have labels or containers representing different kinds of soul food, West Indian food, Chinese food, Italian food, soul music, West Indian music, gospel, etc.) Have available several containers, advertisements, or labels for each item. Be sure to include some items which are enjoyed in general by Americans of different racial and ethnic backgrounds, such as hamburgers, hot dogs, familiar hymns, etc. Arbitrarily assign the same price to each item—for example, one dollar per item. Provide enough play money so that each member of the group can "purchase" ten items. Arrange the different items around the room in which the group meets so that all of the items of the same type are together (for example, all of the soul food items are placed together, all of the Italian food items are placed together, all of the West Indian music items are together, etc.). Put a label where each item is placed, telling what is for sale in that spot.

Step 1—Shopping Trip

1. Give each member of the group enough play money to "purchase" ten items from the store or stores set up around the room.
2. Tell the group how much each item costs.
3. Ask each member of the group to "purchase" from the store(s) the ten items which he or she likes best from what is offered. To "buy" an item, the purchaser takes the container, label, or advertisement representing the item and leaves the correct amount of money in its place.

4. Continue the shopping trip until each person has ten items. Then have the members of the group bring the items they have purchased and gather for the discussion.

Step 2—Discussing the Shopping Trip

1. Have each person in turn show the group what he or she has bought.
2. Ask each person how he or she came to know about or like the things purchased. By having had it in the family? By seeing it in the community? From advertising?
3. By counting the amount of money left at the places where the various items were for sale, determine which items were most popular with the entire group.
4. Summarize the following comments: The things which we choose to buy or do or use tell us a lot about who we are, what we like or dislike, what is important to us. There are many things which influence what we choose and which indirectly, therefore, influence who we are or who we decide to be. What our families, friends, and community feel is important influences what we choose. So does advertisement. Ultimately, it is up to each of us, though, to weigh the various things which influence our choices and decide what we like or dislike, what we will do or buy or use, and what sorts of persons we will be.

Step 3—Does It Fit?

Summarize the following comments: The ancient Israelites, the people of the Old Testament, found that they were very much influenced by the customs and ways of the peoples who lived near them. In the Old Testament the prophets, the servants of God, constantly remind the Israelites that they must not follow the ways of the Canaanites and other peoples who surrounded them, but must remain true to their God and to the laws God had given them. Long before the prophets, however, the Israelites had borrowed from the Canaanites some of their ritual practices and had adapted them for the worship of the God of Israel. Scholars believe that the Israelite practice of offering burnt sacrifices to God was borrowed from the Canaanites. The prophets did not object to this ritual practice as long as those who made the sacrifice sincerely wanted communion with God and forgiveness for their sins and did not feel that their action compelled God to give them these things. It was important that they make their offering to Yahweh, the

Israelite God, and not to Baal, the Canaanite god. When carried out in the correct way, the borrowed rite enabled the Israelites to express their relationship with God in greater fullness than they had been able to before.

There was one part of the Canaanite ritual, however, which the Israelites could not borrow. Under extreme circumstances (for example, when a city was about to fall to an enemy), the Canaanites would sacrifice a human child as a burnt offering. The Israelites knew that child sacrifice had been prohibited in the ancient story of Abraham and Isaac (see Genesis 22:1-14), and they did not believe that such an inhuman act could ever form a part of the worship of the merciful, compassionate One who was their God. Whenever Israelites attempted to imitate the Canaanites by offering their children as burnt sacrifices (see, for example, 2 Kings 17:17; 21:6), they were soundly denounced by others in the Israelite community.

The Israelites, then, could and did choose to borrow some of the customs of the Canaanites and other peoples who surrounded them. But they had always to ask themselves whether or not the custom they chose fit in with who they were and who God had called them to be. Later, as the Jews and the early Christians came into contact with Greek civilization and were influenced by Greek thought and customs, they had to ask the same question: "Does this thought or practice fit in with who I am as a Jew or a Christian?" As each of us tries to decide what is important to him or her, what to buy, or what to do, it is wise to keep in mind the test the Israelites and early Christians—the people of the Bible—used: Does this fit in with who I am and who God calls me to be?

Step 4—Activity: Part of Me

1. Provide everyone with a large sheet of construction paper, scissors, paste or glue, newspapers and magazines, and crayons, paints, or pencils.

2. Have each person make a collage of clippings, drawings, and pictures describing or showing things that he or she likes or finds important.

3. When they have finished, post the collages around the room. Have each person explain his or her collage to the group.

Step 5—Prayer: Being Me

1. Have each person, while looking at his or her collage, imagine that he or she is in the presence of Christ. (Pause)

2. As they, in imagination, present each item of their collages to him, have them ask Christ: "Is this really part of me, or have I chosen it simply because other people like it?" (Pause)

3. Have the youth also ask Christ: "How can these things which I like or find important help me to relate to you?" (Pause) "How can they help me to relate to your people and to the world?" (Pause)

Allow any who wish to share their meditation with the group to do so.

(Step 6—Evaluation)

To evaluate the session with the group, see the suggestions given in Appendix E.

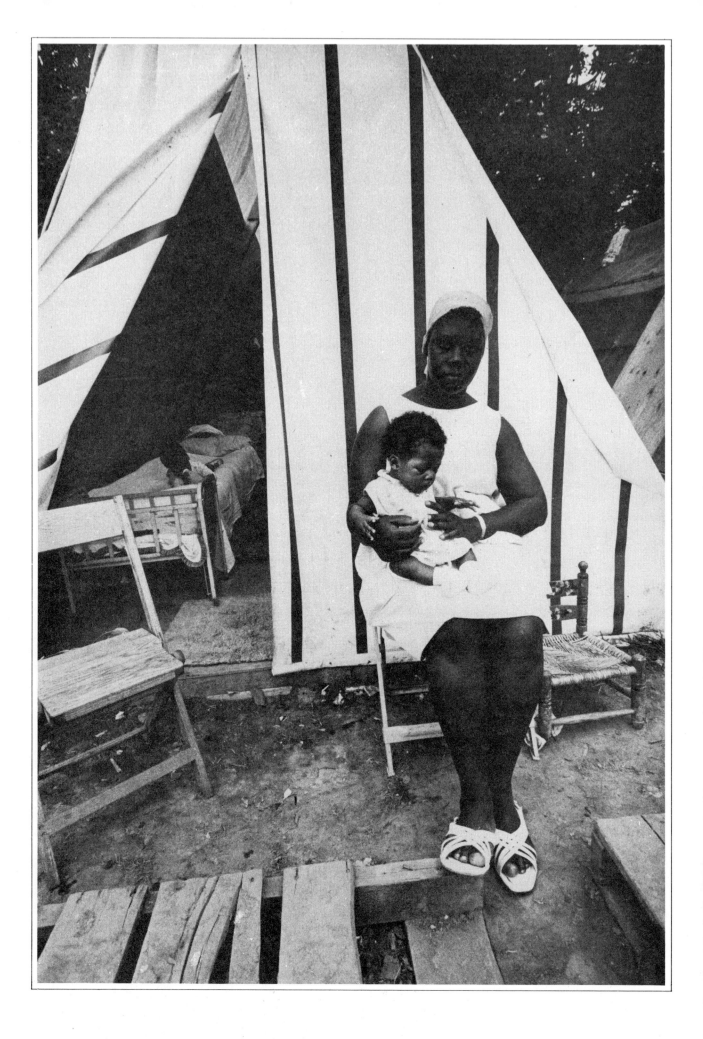

Unit on Suffering, Election, and Mission

—————Background—————

6

The question "Why do I suffer?" is one which has plagued human beings for centuries. In our times more energy has, perhaps, been expended in attempting to answer the question "How do we alleviate suffering?" than in exploring the reasons for it. However, since suffering has played such a large part in our history as black people, the questions "Why do we suffer?" and "What meaning can this suffering have?" have great importance for us.

Session I in this unit shows that all suffering does not come to the sufferer as a punishment from God. It also shows that human beings cannot always understand why God allows them to suffer. In Session II the youth will see that we as black people sometimes inflict suffering on one another. Session III illustrates that others have inflicted suffering on us throughout our history. Throughout the unit, however, suffering, healed and transformed by God, is seen as a potential basis for mission. God has not caused us as a people to suffer as a punishment for sins. God, whose person and will have been revealed through history, seems in *our* history to have elected or chosen us to carry out a mission intimately bound up with our suffering.

In our history, which is one of a people deprived of freedom, justice, and human dignity, God seems to have laid upon us the task of fighting for these things. We have sometimes seen this painful struggle as one which we engaged in because we were black people and were deprived of these basic human rights. However,

this struggle, transformed by God, must continue. It must continue even beyond the time when we individually have obtained these rights. It must continue essentially as the mission of a Christian black people to obtain freedom, justice, and human dignity for all people. Thus, heightened awareness of our condition as a people who have been robbed and preyed upon by others, and of our mission to struggle to obtain justice and dignity for all is presented in Session II as an antidote for preying on one another.

The suffering which we have experienced throughout our history, like that which Christ endured, can be transformed by God to be used by us in and with Christ as a source of blessing and new life for others who still experience suffering. Thus, Sessions I and III provide an opportunity for the youth to present both individual and corporate suffering to God for healing and transformation. They may also begin to envision how these experiences can be used as a source of help for others. Session IV enables the youth to view suffering in ghetto communities. It also enables them to engage in techniques which will be useful in the long-term project.

The suggested social action projects provide an opportunity (1) to make others aware of the suffering which blacks have experienced and of the missions for which these experiences can form the basis after they have been transformed and healed by God or (2) to help those who presently experience suffering.

Grief and Healing

PURPOSE

To enable youth
—to face and explore some of the experiences involved in the grief process
—to envision, if not experience, the healing and transformation possible with grief

OUTLINE OF SESSION

Step 1—Why, Lord?
Step 2—Ted
Step 3—Prayer: Healed and Transformed
Step 4—Activity: "I Ask Your Prayers . . ."
(Step 5—Evaluation)

Step 1—Why, Lord?

Begin the session with this summary and these questions: For thousands of years human beings have wrestled with the problem of suffering. They have wondered why suffering should come to them and what meaning it might have in their lives. The story of Job in the Bible tells us something of one man's experience with suffering.

Job was both a very wealthy man and a very devout and religious one. He had a large family, many servants, and many cattle and other livestock. He was so wealthy that his children were able to have many feasts and parties. But all of that was to come to an end.

1. Read or have the group read Job 1:6–2:13. Then ask these questions:

2. "What happened to Job, to his family, and all of his wealth?" (His children were killed; his livestock were stolen and struck by lightning; his servants were killed; Job was afflicted with an illness; and even his wife seemed to turn against him.)

3. "Who caused this suffering to come upon Job?" (God allowed Satan to cause Job to suffer as a test.)

4. "Did this suffering come to Job because he had sinned?" (No.)

5. "Why did God allow Satan to cause Job to suffer?" (To see whether, as Satan claimed, Job would curse God if he lost all the blessings he had formerly enjoyed.)

6. "Did Job curse God when he had lost everything?" (No.)

Continue with the following comments: Although we know that Job's suffering was not brought about because he sinned, neither Job nor his three friends knew this. As his suffering continued, Job cried out.

7. Read or have the group read Job 7:11-19 and 10:1-3. Then ask these questions:

8. "What does Job say God is doing to him?" (Hounding him day and night, oppressing and condemning him, giving him no rest.)

9. "How does Job seem to feel about God at this point? Is he happy with God, angry with God, questioning what God is doing, or what?" (Job seems to be angry with God and questioning what God is doing.)

10. "Does Job still believe in God, or has he given up on God and decided that God is no longer relevant to his life?" (He still believes in God and feels that God is important for his life, although he may question what God is doing.)

Continue: Job's so-called friends answered him.

11. Read or have the group read Job 11:1-6; 22:1, 22-25. Then ask these questions:

12. "Why do the friends think Job is suffering?" (The friends think that Job is suffering because he has sinned against God.)

13. "What do they seem to think will happen if Job admits his sin?" (They think God will give Job riches again if he admits his sin.)

Continue: But Job answers his friends.

14. Read or have the group read Job 13:13-18; 16:1-5; and 23:1-12. Then ask these questions:

15. "Does Job believe that he has sinned?" (No.)

16. "Does Job think that the friends are right in saying to him what they are saying?" (No.)

17. "How does he think friends should behave toward someone who is experiencing misfortune?" (He thinks a friend should comfort someone who is in distress and try to lessen his or her grief.)

Continue: Job demanded that God answer him and show him why he was being made to suffer since he had not sinned. And God does speak to Job.

18. Read or have the group read Job 38:1-13 and 40:1-14.

19. "Does God tell Job why he is suffering?" (No.)

20. "Does God say that Job has sinned?" (No.)

Continue: Essentially God tells Job that the understanding and ways of God are so much greater than that of human beings that Job can neither understand why suffering has come to him nor dispute with God. But because he had experienced suffering and had dared to question what meaning that suffering could have for his life, Job learned something from his experience.

21. Read or have the group read Job 42:1-10. Then

ask these questions:

22. "What did Job learn from his experience?" (He came to know God from his own personal experience, as he had not known God before, and he came to realize that God's ways could not be encompassed by human understanding.)

23. "What does God say about Job's friends? Were they right in speaking to Job as they had and in assuming that Job's suffering was a punishment for sin?" (No.)

Continue: Suffering, of course, did not stop with Job. It is something that we still have with us.

Step 2—Ted

Read or have someone read the following case history to the group and then continue with the questions for discussion.

Ted

Ted lived with his grandmother and grandfather in a house in the city. Although Ted had two brothers and three sisters, Ted was the only one who lived with Grandmother and Grandfather.

On Saturdays during the summer Ted and Grandfather would go fishing together, and sometimes in the evenings, Grandpa would tell Ted about what it was like when he was a boy.

Ted had a good friend, Randy, who lived around the corner. Sometimes after school Ted would go with Randy and Randy's dog, Zeek, to the park, and Randy would throw a stick for Zeek to catch. Randy was an only child, and he loved Zeek almost as if he were a human being. At one time Zeek had gone along everywhere with Randy, even when Grandpa took Ted and Randy fishing. But Zeek was getting old now and could not get around as much as he used to.

It was the first Saturday in the summer vacation, and Ted was anxious to go fishing with Grandpa. Randy was not going with them this time. Last week Zeek had died, and Randy could not yet bring himself to go fishing without his faithful dog.

Ted wondered what was taking Grandpa so long. Slowly, Ted's grandfather came into the living room.

"I don't think I'm going to stay out too long," he said, "but I sure don't want to miss going; so let's get moving."

The fish were really biting that day. Ted got one of the biggest fish he'd ever caught.

When they got home, Ted's grandfather went straight to his bedroom and called for Ted's grandmother to come to him. A short while later Ted's grandmother came to the door and said, "Grandpa isn't feeling too good. I think we'd better get Mr. Jones around the corner to help us take him to the hospital."

At the hospital the doctor said that Grandpa was very sick, that he had had a stroke and would have to stay in the hospital. The doctor explained that high blood pressure caused people to have strokes. More black people than white people have high blood pressure, and thus black people who are middle-aged and older ought to have their blood pressure checked often. The doctor said, also, that Grandpa had probably had very high blood pressure for a long time and could have had a stroke at any time.

Ted and his grandmother didn't come home from the hospital until late that night. When Ted got home, he sat down on his bed to think. He didn't want Grandpa to die. He wanted to go fishing with him some more, and he wanted to sit next to him and hear him tell about when he was a boy.

"Please, God," he prayed, "don't let my grandfather die."

Ted woke up with a start as the telephone rang. He ran to get the telephone, but his grandmother had already answered it. When she finished talking, she turned to Ted.

"That was the hospital," she said. "They said that Grandpa died about fifteen minutes ago."

Over the next few days Ted's mother and aunts and uncles and sisters and brothers all arrived. And many of his grandmother's and grandfather's friends came by, too. After Ted and his grandmother had come home from the funeral and had eaten, Randy came to the door. Ted sat down outside with him.

"I just wanted to tell you I'm sorry your grandfather died," Randy said. "I can sort of understand how you feel. Like, although Zeek wasn't really a person or anything like that, I felt bad when he died, because ever since I can remember, we'd had Zeek.

"Man, I cried some, and Mom and Dad cried, too. We all cried just over an old dog!"

"I wish I knew how I feel about Grandpa dying," Ted replied. "Sometimes I get mad about the whole thing—mad at the hospital people, mad at God, mad at everybody. If those jive doctors over at the hospital had worked a little harder, maybe Grandpa would be alive right now. But they don't really care when somebody black comes in.

"And look, man, I *prayed* that God would make Grandpa well, and God didn't do it. Why'd God have to take Grandpa away? God knew I loved Grandpa! Besides, Grandpa probably wouldn't even have been sick if God had made him white instead of black. The doctor said that most of the people who get high blood pressure and have strokes are black. Why does everything have to happen to black people?"

Ted paused.

"Sometimes I feel like I killed him. I mean, if I hadn't

been so hot on going fishing that day, maybe he'd still be alive. I should have known he didn't feel good. That's why he was so slow getting ready. But, no, I had to go fishing! I don't think I'll ever go fishing again!"

"Gee, I don't think your Grandpa would want you to quit fishing," Randy replied. "I mean, I think he would want you to go get those big ones, just for him. I know it's hard to go down there, though, without him. Mom says when someone or something you love dies, you feel bad for a long time.

"I've been thinking," Randy continued, "that I might sign up to be a fishing buddy with the Boys Club. You know, you can sign up to take a little boy fishing, teach him to cast and how to bait the hook and things like that. I thought I'd sign up for a Saturday near the end of August. Maybe you'd like to go, too."

"Yeah," said Ted. "Maybe so."

The boys sat for a short while longer. Then Randy went home, and Ted got up and went inside.

The summer went by slowly. Just before the last Saturday in August, Randy came by to remind Ted of the Boys Club fishing buddy program, and Ted agreed to go fishing with Randy and two little boys that Saturday.

On Saturday Ted tried hard to remember to tell the little boys all his grandfather had taught him. And he tried to be as gentle and patient as his grandfather had been—even when they got their lines tangled into a thousand knots.

Ted still missed his grandfather. But as the weeks passed, he began to look forward to going fishing with the boys from the Boys Club. He still didn't know why God had let Grandpa die, but he did know that as a result of his grief and his desire to be like his grandfather, he was learning to be gentle and patient and to share his love with some people he might otherwise never have even known.

Discussion Questions

1. Do you think that it was right for Ted to question why God allowed Grandfather to die? If so, why? If not, why not? (Yes. The story of Job shows us that it was by questioning why he was experiencing suffering that Job was able to know God better and have his experience transformed into something that was meaningful for his life.)

2. Do you think that Ted contributed to his grandfather's death by going fishing with him on the day that he died? If so, why? If not, why not? (No. Grandfather could have made the decision to stay at home even though Ted had wanted to go fishing. Grandfather had apparently wanted to go fishing.)

3. Do you think that it was natural for Ted to feel guilty for what happened to his grandfather? (Yes.

People often feel guilty when someone they love dies, but that doesn't mean that they contributed to the person's death in any way.)

4. Do you think that it was natural for Ted to feel angry with the doctors and angry with God because his grandfather died? If so, why? If not, why not? (Yes. Job also was angry with God in his suffering. Anger is a response that many people have when they experience suffering, especially if they feel that they don't deserve to suffer.)

5. Do you think that God is punishing black people by allowing them to be more likely to have high blood pressure than whites? If so, why? If not, why not? (No. The Job story shows us that all suffering does not come as a punishment for sin and that we cannot always understand why we are allowed to suffer.)

6. Did Ted ever learn why he had to suffer? (No.)

7. How was Ted's experience of suffering transformed to become a constructive and meaningful part of his life? (Ted was able to begin to incorporate parts of his grandfather's personality and to share the skills his grandfather had taught him with others.)

Step 3—Prayer: Healed and Transformed

Give the following comment: None of us goes out to look for suffering, but much of the suffering and the feelings that we experience because of suffering can be healed by God and transformed into something meaningful, useful, and constructive for ourselves and others. Although it is natural to feel guilty or angry or despairing or sad for a while after one has experienced great suffering and loss, when these feelings remain very intense, they can make it impossible to use the experience in a constructive way for ourselves or others. When these feelings have been healed and transformed by Christ, we can use our own painful experience as the basis for developing an understanding, compassion, and concern which will be of help to others who suffer.

1. Have the youth imagine that they are in the presence of Christ. (Pause)

2. Have them recall some personal experience of suffering or, if they have not personally experienced suffering, have them recall an experience which happened to someone close to them. (Pause)

3. Ask the youth to try to feel again how they felt at that time. (If they are recalling someone else's experience, have them imagine how the person felt at that time.) (Pause)

4. Have them imagine that they are presenting these feelings to Christ and asking him to heal them. (Pause)

5. Have the members of the group try to imagine how Christ might transform the experience of suffering that they have recalled so that it can become useful,

constructive, and meaningful for themselves and others. (Pause)

Allow those who wish to discuss their meditation with the group to do so.

Step 4—Activity: "I Ask Your Prayers . . ."

1. Pass out to the group members paper, pens, crayons or paint, recent newspapers and magazines, scissors, and glue.

2. Have the members of the group cut out of the newspapers and magazines articles and pictures on situations which involve suffering (such as articles on accidents, natural disasters, crime, etc.). Have them also write short reports on people whom they know who are experiencing suffering (are sick, have had a loved one die, are going through a divorce, etc.). Names of the persons involved can be excluded from the reports, if you wish.

3. Paste the articles, pictures, and reports on a board or a large sheet of cardboard or stiff paper entitled, "I Ask Your Prayers."

4. Place the board near the entrance of the church building. Ask members of the congregation and others who come to the church building to use the board as a reminder to pray for the persons and conditions described or pictured on the board.

(Step 5—Evaluation)

To evaluate the session with the group, see the suggestions given in Appendix E.

Taking Care of Business

PURPOSE

To enable youth
—to examine an instance where suffering is brought on members of the black community by other blacks
—to explore a biblical example of the same kind of experience
—to explore ways to remedy this situation

OUTLINE OF SESSION

Step 1—Robert OR Delbert
Step 2—Ezra and the People Rebuild
Step 3—Prayer: Bearing One Another's Burdens
Step 4—Activity: Respond!
(Step 5—Evaluation)

Step 1—(Alternative A) Robert

Read or tell the group the following case history.

Robert

Robert crouched in an alley in a dark, lonely inner-city block.

"Nice," thought Robert.

He was waiting. Seemed like he always had to wait for old folks. Of course, the ones with canes walked even more slowly than the rest, but that was the kind he liked. Some of them could barely stand up as it was, and here they'd come tip-tipping down the street. He could hit them, grab the purse or wallet, and be gone before they even knew what happened. They'd be all sprawled out on the street. He never really had to worry about getting caught with that kind. It would be a half-hour before they could even get up off of the sidewalk!

He remembered waiting for his mom when he was a kid. He'd wait for her to come out of the bar, or out of her room, or wherever it was she was drinking so maybe she'd give him some money to go to the store and get a bag of potato chips or something for dinner. He didn't dare go in to ask her for anything. She'd hit him and curse him out. Tell him, "You aren't worth nothing, just like your father, just like all black men." And then she wouldn't give him a penny!

Well, he was never going to wait around just to ASK someone for money anymore. He'd TAKE. It ought to be his anyway. What are old folks, shuffling or tip-tipping down the street on a cane and shaking all over and moving like they're on their last legs, going to do with money anyway? Like, they're not going to be

going somewhere or really *doing* something with it.

From down the street Robert could hear coming toward him the slow, shuffling steps of an old man. In just a few minutes he wouldn't have to wait anymore.

After reading the case history, use these questions for discussion:

1. "How do you feel about Robert?" (Angry? Sympathetic? Think he's dreadful? Or confused?)

2. "Why do you think he robs elderly crippled people?" (Because he thinks he won't get caught? Because he's persuaded himself that they don't need money? He hates older people because they remind him of his mother?)

3. "Is Robert right in believing that older people have nothing to do with their money?" (No.) "What are some of the things older people need money for?" (Food, housing, medical care, clothing, etc.)

4. "How do Robert and others like him affect inner-city black communities?" (They cause a lot of suffering. Those who rob the elderly cause them both physical and financial hardship since the elderly in inner-city neighborhoods often have available only small, fixed incomes to take care of their basic needs.)

5. "Why doesn't Robert care about how he affects others in the black community?" (Because he's had to look out for himself for so long that he doesn't care about others? Because he feels that other people owe him something?)

Step 1—(Alternative B) Delbert

1. Divide the group into two groups.

2. Give or tell each of the groups one of the role plays printed below.

3. Ask the members of each group to discuss the questions at the end of their role play among themselves.

4. Read Role Play #1 aloud. Then ask the group that discussed Role Play #1 to act out both the role-play information and what they think the players will do at the end of the situation. Have them also explain how they think the persons involved feel.

5. Ask the members of the other group to explain why they agree or disagree with what Group #1 presented.

6. Repeat 4 and 5 for Group #2 with Role Play #2.

Role Play #1

Mr. and Mrs. Johnson are an elderly couple. Mr.

Johnson is nearly blind, and Mrs. Johnson is badly crippled with arthritis. Neither of them can work anymore. Every month they receive a small check from the government. As usually happens, this month they ran out of money before the next check was due. However, they had received a letter from their son with thirty dollars in it. Mr. Johnson had gone off to the store with the letter containing the money, but he dropped it on the way. He doesn't know where he dropped it and can't see well enough to find it. He has just returned home and told his wife what happened. How do you think the Johnsons feel? What do you think they will do?

Role Play #2

Delbert lives with his mother and three sisters in a black inner-city neighborhood. One day as Delbert is walking down the street, he sees an envelope lying on the ground. He picks it up. The envelope had been mailed to Mr. and Mrs. Willie Johnson, who live down the street. Delbert doesn't know the Johnsons very well. They are old people, and Delbert doesn't like to bother with old people too much.

The envelope has already been opened, and so Delbert looks inside. There is a letter inside with three ten-dollar bills in it. Delbert quickly puts the money in his pocket and drops the envelope in the trash can. Down the street he sees Mrs. Johnson slowly coming down the steps from her house. She stops and begins to poke her cane into the leaves around the doorstep. How do you think Delbert feels? What do you think he will do?

After the role plays, ask the entire group this question:

7. "If Delbert had known the Johnsons' situation and how they felt about losing the money, what do you think he would have done when he saw the envelope?" (Returned it to them? Spent the money himself even though he knew that they had very little money?)

Step 2—Ezra and the People Rebuild

Summarize the following comments: The crime rate in black inner-city communities is quite high. In many cases it is people from the community who prey on their neighbors and cause them great suffering. As blacks, we are not the only ones ever to bring suffering on our own people. The ancient Israelites also had the same problem.

In 587 B.C., the city of Jerusalem was captured and destroyed by the Babylonians; and the Judeans, the Israelites who lived around Jerusalem, were taken as slaves to Babylonia. Earlier, other Israelite peoples had also been conquered and carried away as slaves. For years before these disasters struck, God had sent prophets to the Israelites. The prophets had told the people that they had turned away from God. In some cases Israelite men had married foreign wives and had begun to worship their wives' gods. In other cases the Israelites had simply uncritically begun to copy the ways of the people who surrounded them. The prophets had warned that the Israelite kingdoms would be destroyed if the people did not return to the true worship of their own God. But the people did not listen.

By 538 B.C., when the captives in Babylonia were allowed to return to their homeland, many of the returning leaders were convinced that their people had been defeated and made slaves because they had turned from God. They felt that the people had brought great suffering on themselves and were determined that this should not happen again.

Life was extremely hard for those who returned to Jerusalem. The city was in ruins, and food was scarce. Because the surrounding peoples had begun to harass them, the Israelites built a wall around the city to protect themselves. But there were other threats to their security. In the following passage Ezra writes of this threat.

1. Divide the youth into two groups, the members of one imagining that they are Ezra and the members of the other that they are Israelites with foreign wives.

2. Read Ezra 9:1-2, 10-12. Then ask the group representing Ezra how they think Ezra felt when he heard these things. (Sad, fearful that the people might be enslaved again, etc.)

3. Read Ezra 10:1-5, 9-11. Ask the group representing the Israelites with foreign wives how they would feel hearing Ezra's decree. (Sad that they must leave their wives and children.)

4. Ask the group representing Israelites with foreign wives what it might say to Ezra, and ask the Ezra group what it might reply to the Israelites with foreign wives.

5. Ask everyone: "Why do you think Ezra did what he did?" (To prevent the people from bringing suffering on themselves again.)

6. What did Ezra hope to accomplish by having only Israelites in the Israelite community? (He thought Israelites would be less tempted to follow the ways of other people and would be faithful to the God of Israel if their communities were restricted to Israelites.)

Comment: "Ezra tried to instill in his people a strong sense of nationhood, or community, and remind them of their mission to be a pure and holy people, different from the other peoples of the world. He apparently felt that he had to use very drastic means to bring this about. To help promote a strong sense of nationhood, unity, and purpose and to insure their survival in a hostile environment, Ezra forcefully created a community composed only of those who shared a common racial heritage and who, because of this heritage, shared a common belief and purpose as well. By stressing these common factors and by excluding all who did not share them, Ezra hoped to prevent his people from bringing suffering again upon themselves. Of course, even within this circumscribed community there were factors which caused people to differ from one another—factors which could have been used to bring about disunity, internal strife and weakness, and the eventual fall of the nation again. Some Israelites were old and some were young; some, like Ezra and the priests and the princes, held positions of greater power and authority than others did. However, Ezra felt that these lesser differences could be overcome if the people could unite to carry out the mission which God had laid upon them.

"Even though God has not caused us as black people to suffer as a punishment for sin, God, whose person and will have been revealed through history, seems in our history to have laid on us or elected or chosen us to carry out a mission that is intimately bound up with our suffering. For us blacks in the United States, our skin color and other easily recognizable Negroid physical characteristics have caused us to share a common history. This history is one of a people who were preyed on by others who, especially during the eras of slavery and segregation, robbed us of the rewards which we should have received for our labor, of opportunity and a sense of self-worth, and of freedom and justice. Throughout our history we have had in common the painful struggle to obtain freedom, justice, and human dignity. We have often seen this painful struggle as one which we were engaged in because we were black people and were deprived of these basic human rights. But to participate in the struggle to 'set the downtrodden free' (Luke 4:18), to 'establish justice' (Isaiah 42:4) and to promote human dignity for all (see Acts 10:28b, 34) is to participate in the mission of Christ. Thus, we are called to continue this struggle along with Christ on behalf of all people as essentially the mission of a *Christian* black people.

"As with the people of Ezra's time, there are factors which cause us to differ from one another. Some of us are old and some are young; some are poor and inadequately trained, while others are a little more affluent and have received a good education. However, a heightened awareness of our condition as a people who have been robbed and preyed on by others and of our mission to struggle to obtain freedom, justice, and dignity for all can, perhaps, help us to stop inflicting suffering on one another."

Step 3—Prayer: Bearing One Another's Burdens

Summarize this opening comment: Being aware that people still suffer and learning to empathize with them, to experience within ourselves what they are feeling, can help prepare us to overcome our differences and unite to continue our struggle for freedom, justice, and human dignity for all.

1. Have the members of the group imagine that they are in the presence of Christ. (Pause)

2. Have them ask Christ to help them in their imagination to meet and empathize with each of the people in the situations in the Justice unit, Session III, Step 3 (see pages 64-65). Read each situation through slowly. However, instead of asking the questions which come at the end of the situation as printed, make the following statements:

3. After Situation #1: "Try to feel as Joereen felt." (Pause) (Repeat for the other three situations.)

4. Have the members of the group ask Christ to bless those who are experiencing suffering and to keep us mindful of them. (Pause)

Allow any who wish to discuss their meditation with the group to do so.

Step 4—Activity: Respond!

1. Have available a large sheet of poster board which can be used as the background for a collage.

2. Pass out magazines, newspapers, scissors, pencils, crayons or paints, paper, and glue.

3. Ask the members of the group to cut out of the newspapers and magazines (or to draw) pictures of people which would evoke some response in those who see them (for example, the picture of a baby crying might cause someone to respond by picking up the child; the picture of a hungry person might cause someone to respond by providing food or money to buy food).

4. After all the pictures have been prepared, assign each one a number and have the members of the group write that number on the picture.

5. Arrange and paste the pictures on the poster board or cardboard to form an attractive collage.

6. The collage will be placed in a visible place in the church building, and those who enter the church will be invited to make some response to the pictures. Be sure to include with the collage a pad and pencil for the responses and instructions asking those who pass by to look at the pictures and write on the pad the number of the picture to which they are responding and the response they would make.

(Step 5—Evaluation)

To evaluate the session with the group, see the suggestions given in Appendix E.

"Here Is My Servant, My Chosen"

PURPOSE

To enable youth

—to know and experience some of the suffering which blacks have encountered here in the United States

—to see the suffering of blacks in relationship to the sufferings of Christ

—to understand that suffering can be transformed and used for good

OUTLINE OF SESSION

Step 1—Captured! OR The Turn of the Century OR "We Shall Overcome"

Step 2—"He Was Oppressed and He Was Afflicted"

Step 3—Prayer: "And with His Stripes We Are Healed"

Step 4—Activity: "The Crippled Child"

(Step 5—Evaluation)

Step 1—(Alternative A) Captured!

Divide into groups of two. In each group of two, one person is the slave and the other is the captor (in scene 1) and slave driver (in scene 2). In scene 1 the captor captures the slave and forces him or her to stand for a short time with arms raised overhead as though he or she were chained. In scene 2 the slave works bent over, as though tending a crop. The slave driver makes certain that the slave does not slow down or stop work. After both scenes have been played, the two switch roles (the slave becomes the captor/slave driver, and the captor/slave driver becomes the slave) and play the two scenes again.

Discussion

1. "How did you feel when, as the slave, your arms were chained overhead?" (It hurt, did not like it; perhaps, were angry with the captor.)

2. "Suppose that, as the captor, you had been told that you would get a lot of money for every slave that you captured but that you would get nothing if the slave got away. As the captor, how would you feel as you stood watching the slaves with their arms chained overhead?" (Fearful that the slaves might get away, anxious to collect your money, happy to have collected your money, etc.)

3. "How would you feel if you really had to work as a slave, bent over in the fields all day long without any pay?" (Painful, tired, stiff, angry, sad, etc.)

4. "Suppose that, as the slave driver, you were paid according to how much the slaves produced: if they produce a lot, you are paid a lot; if they produce a little, you are paid a little. How would you behave toward them?" (Force them to produce a lot; not allow them to rest, etc.)

5. "If you had been a slave, chained with your hands above your head after your capture and forced to work bent over all day in the fields without much rest, how do you think you would behave toward other slaves if you were suddenly made the slave driver?" (More kindly, perhaps; or, perhaps, just as anxious as any other slave driver to make money or to do well in your new job.)

Step 1 (Alternative B) The Turn of the Century

Read or tell the following story of Booker T. Washington to the group. For the first role play, choose three people to play the roles of the three characters involved, and divide the group into three groups, one to support each of the three characters. The group members supporting the person playing Booker T. Washington will tell him how they think Booker T. Washington would have reacted in the situation and help him answer the discussion question directed toward him. The other two support groups will advise their persons as to how to answer the questions directed to their characters.

Booker T. Washington was born a slave. When the Civil War was over and the slaves were freed, he moved to West Virginia with his family. As a boy, he worked in the mines. He also went to school because he had always been eager to learn. He saved his money and finally went to Hampton Institute. After graduating from Hampton, he taught there for a while. Then he founded Tuskegee Institute in Alabama. Tuskegee Institute was supported by several white millionaires in the North. Washington had obtained their help by showing them what his hard work and the hard work of his students had achieved.

Washington felt that any black could do what he had done if he or she worked hard and did not become lazy. But at that time black people did not have many rights. Even though it is not true, many people believed that black people are inferior to white people and should not have the same rights. Blacks could not eat in certain places or go to school or even go to the theaters with whites, and many blacks were being killed by mobs of white people.

Booker T. Washington did not believe that blacks should fight for justice by protesting these unfair laws. He thought that blacks should just study and work quietly. He felt that hard work would change things but that protest would only make things worse.

Washington had hoped that many white people who had power would fight for justice for blacks if blacks showed themselves to be good people by working hard. But he did not realize that, at the time, justice for blacks was not very important to very many white people who had power.

Role Play #1

One day Booker T. Washington was walking to school when he saw a white woman down the road. She was with her black maid who was trying to carry some wood. The maid was having trouble because there was too much wood for her to carry, and the white woman would not help.

When the woman saw Washington, she said, "Hey, boy, help my maid carry this wood." Washington was not a boy. He was a grown man and president of Tuskegee Institute! How do you think he would have reacted?

Discussion

Have the entire group decide whether or not the person who was to react as Washington would have reacted did so correctly. Have the group explain why the performance was or was not correct. Then ask these questions.

1. Ask the person who played the white woman: "How did you feel about the maid when she was having trouble carrying the wood?" (Sorry for the maid, angry with her because she was slowing things up, etc.) "How did you feel when you saw Booker T. Washington?" (That there was another one of those people who is supposed to do that kind of work; that he should be helping me.)

2. Ask the person who played the maid: "If you were really the black maid, how would you feel when Booker T. Washington was told to carry the wood?" (Embarrassed, saddened that an older black man was not respected?) "How would you feel when he reacted as he did?" (Perhaps contemptuous, that he should give in so easily; or perhaps relieved, that he hadn't tried to make trouble.)

3. Ask the person who played Washington: "If you were really Booker T. Washington, president of Tuskegee Institute, how would you have felt when the woman called you a boy and told you to help her maid?" (Sorry for the woman because she hadn't learned to treat black people as equals; sad because white people were not yet able to accept black people;

angry because the maid was not working hard enough and was making the woman think that black people are lazy.) "If you yourself had grown up to be an important man and a woman had called you a boy and told you to help her maid, how would you have felt?" (Angry because the woman showed no respect for you and what you had achieved. Perhaps some of the responses listed above for the first part of the question.)

4. If the responses from the maid indicated contempt or disgust with Washington or if those from the person playing Washington indicated anger with the woman, point this out to the group and ask: "Do you think many black people may have felt that way? If so, do you think that black people could continue for a long time behaving as Washington advised, since many of them may have had these feelings? What sorts of things might make them continue to behave as Washington advised in spite of their feelings?"

For the second role play, choose people to act the part of the characters involved and have three support groups, as before, to guide and advise the three groups of characters: Booker T. Washington, the two white boys, and the two black boys.

Role Play #2

One afternoon two black boys about twelve years old were walking down the street. Coming toward them were two white boys about the same age. The two white boys began calling the black boys names, and one of them picked up a rock and threw it at them. The black boys did not know what to do. Booker T. Washington saw the whole thing. He walked over to the black boys. What do you think he would have told them to do?

Discussion

Have the entire group decide whether or not the person who played Washington did what he would have done. If the performance was correct, why? If not, why not? Then ask these questions.

1. Ask the people who played the two white boys: "If you were walking down the street in your neighborhood and saw two boys you did not know coming toward you, what might you feel about them?" (Curious—who are they? Happy—here are two new boys to get to know? Angry—what are they doing on my street? Mischievous—I bet I can tease those boys? Frightened—will they try to hurt me?) "Now, if you were two white boys who lived when Booker T. Washington lived, how do you think you might have felt seeing two black boys walking down the street?" (There are two kids I can bother and they'd better not bother me? What are *those* kids doing around here?)

2. Ask the youth who played the two black boys: "If you were walking down the street in your neighborhood and two boys began throwing rocks at you and calling you names, what would you have done?" (Tried to make them stop, perhaps fought them?) "Now, if you were two black boys who lived when Booker T. Washington lived, how do you think you might have felt seeing two white boys walking down the street toward you?" (Frightened—will they try to hurt me?) "How would you have felt after Booker T. Washington told you what to do?" (Angry at him, because he wouldn't let you fight? Confused, because you weren't sure that what he told you to do would work?)

3. Ask the youth who played Booker T. Washington: "If you were just any adult (not Booker T. Washington) and you saw some boys throwing rocks at some other boys and calling them names, what would you do?" (Make the boys stop throwing rocks and calling names? Explain to the boys who were throwing rocks and calling names that they could hurt the other boys? Take the delinquent boys to their parents, if they refused to stop? Try to help all the boys become friends?) "How would you have felt?" (Angry that they were misbehaving? Fearful that the boys might hurt one another? Anxious that they all become friends?) "If you were Booker T. Washington, how might you have felt if you saw two white boys throwing rocks at the two black boys and calling them names?" (Sad because white people were still bothering black people.)

4. If the youth playing the two black boys indicated that they would have been angry or confused, or if the person playing Washington said that he would have been angry with the boys throwing rocks had he been just any adult, point this out to the group and ask: "Do you think many black people may have felt that way? If so, do you think that black people could continue for a long time behaving as Washington advised, since many of them may have had these feelings? What sorts of things might make them continue to behave as Washington advised in spite of their feelings?" (Fear of physical violence against them; fear that they might lose a job or otherwise be harmed; belief that they were, in fact, inferior to whites.)

Now read or tell the group the story of W. E. B. Du Bois (below), choose persons to enact the role plays, divide the group into support groups, and discuss the role plays as done before.

W. E. B. Du Bois lived at the same time as Booker T. Washington did, but he grew up very differently. Du Bois was born in Massachusetts after the Civil War. He grew up and went to school with the boys in his small town. These boys were mostly white.

After high school Du Bois went to Fisk University. It was there that he began to love his people, black people, and their history, songs, and stories. He also became aware of the unfair conditions in which black people were forced to live.

After graduating from Fisk, he studied at Harvard University. Then he studied in Germany for two years. When he returned to the United States, he did work in different cities.

Du Bois was a well-educated man. He got very upset with the conditions for black people. He felt that black people had to demand justice if they were ever to have self-respect and the respect of others. He felt that hard work was important but that it was not the only answer. Unity was what he thought black people needed. If black people had unity and demanded their rights, he thought things would change.

Many white people did not like Du Bois's idea of what black people should do. The whites knew, however, that they did not have to listen if black people demanded justice. Black people were not strong enough to obtain what they demanded. Du Bois formed the National Association for the Advancement of Colored People. Though he worked through that organization to obtain the right to a fair trial, laws against lynching, and voting rights for blacks, it was years later that any of these things came to pass

Role Play #3

Du Bois was going to the library to do some research. When he reached the library door, he saw a sign that read No Negroes Allowed. He went in anyway. A white librarian said to him, "The sign said no Negroes! Now get out and don't start any trouble." Some of the books that Du Bois had written were on the shelves in that library! How do you think Du Bois might have reacted?

Discussion

Have the group decide whether or not the person who played Du Bois did what he would have done. If the performance was correct, why? If not, why not? Then ask these questions.

1. Ask the person who played the librarian: "If you had been a white person living when Du Bois lived and Du Bois came into the library, how might you have felt?" (Oh, dear, here comes a troublemaker. Why don't those people stay where they belong?)

2. Ask the person who played Du Bois: "Had you been Du Bois, how would you have felt when you saw the sign at the library and when the librarian told you to leave?" (Angry, outraged, feeling that this injustice should not be allowed to pass.)

3. Ask the group: "What were the possible conse-

quences if Du Bois had acted as you just showed?" (It depends, of course, on what action the person chose as likely for Du Bois. If Du Bois had refused to leave the library, the librarian may have called the police, who may have removed him and warned him not to go back again, or jailed him for trespassing; or a white crowd may even have lynched him. Had Du Bois tried to encourage other blacks to stage a protest, he may have found few blacks willing to participate because they feared reprisals. Even if he had been able to stage a protest, it may not have brought about change because there would not be enough whites with power willing to help.) Ask: "If these were the probable consequences, do you think that many blacks would continue to behave as Du Bois advised?"

Role Play #4

A black youth and his girl friend were walking home from hearing Booker T. Washington and W. E. B. Du Bois speak. They were talking about the differences between the two men. Two white youth came over and began teasing the black girl. Show what the black youth might have done if he acted as Du Bois had advised black people to act.

Discussion

Have the group decide whether or not the person who played the black youth reacted as Du Bois had advised. If the performance had been correct, why? If not, why not? Then ask these questions.

1. Ask those playing the two white youths: "If you had been a white youth living when Du Bois lived, what might you have felt when you saw the black youth and his girl friend walking down the street?" (There's someone I can bother who wouldn't dare bother me.)

2. Ask the person who played the black girl: "If you had been a black girl living when Du Bois lived and were walking down the street with your boyfriend, how would you have felt when the white boys began to tease you?" (Frightened that they might hurt you and frightened that they might hurt him.)

3. Ask the person who played the black youth: "If you had been a black youth living when Du Bois lived, how would you have felt when two white boys began to tease your girl friend?" (Angry, frightened for both yourself and for your girl friend.)

4. Ask the entire group: "What were the possible consequences if the youth had acted as was just shown?" (It depends on what the person chose as likely behavior for the youth. If the black youth confronted the two youth who were teasing his girl friend, they might ignore him or beat him up. If the black youth attempted to fight the two white youth, they would most probably beat him, and they might rape the girl as

well if they felt they could get away with both actions.) "If these were the probable consequences, do you think that many blacks would act as Du Bois advised?"

Step 1—(Alternative C) "We Shall Overcome"

Begin with the following: "Martin Luther King, Jr., was a black man who was born and grew up in the southern part of the U.S. during the time when there was legal segregation. With segregation there were laws which said that black people could not go to school with white people, eat in the same restaurants, stay in the same hotels, play in the same playgrounds. Blacks had to use separate areas in buses and trains and in hospitals and even in graveyards. After King grew up, he went to the North to study to become a minister. Then he returned to the South and became the minister of the Dexter Avenue Baptist Church in Montgomery, Alabama. Here is an incident which happened while he was there."

Read or tell or have someone who reads well read aloud the following story.

"One day while Martin Luther King was living in Montgomery, a black woman named Rosa Parks got on a bus. She had worked all day, and she was tired. She sat down in a seat. Soon the bus was full of passengers. A white man got on. There were no more seats left. By custom black people were supposed to get up to let a white person sit down. When the bus driver asked Mrs. Parks to get up, she refused. The bus driver called the police, and they arrested Mrs. Parks.

"The Montgomery Improvement Association formed in support of Mrs. Parks. The Reverend Martin Luther King, Jr., was made the president. The Montgomery Improvement Association called for a boycott of the buses until the bus line had done away with the segregated practices. Black people refused to ride the buses for one year. Finally, the buses were integrated."

Role Play #1

Now set up chairs in rows as though they were seats in a bus. Have members of the group act out the incident. Have them make up dialogue that they think might have been spoken. You may want to show in some way which youth are "white" and which are "black." Have the "blacks" sitting in the back of the bus before the action starts. In the first scene, act out the confrontation between Rosa Parks and the bus driver. In the second scene show the bus empty and the "black" people walking past it. Perhaps the "white" bus driver taunts them or invites them to ride, but the blacks pay no attention to him. In the third scene "blacks" and "whites" are riding in the bus seated wherever they want. Follow this drama with these questions.

Discussion

1. Ask the person who played Rosa Parks: "How did you feel when the bus driver insisted that you give up your seat and then called the police to arrest you when you refused?" (Frightened, tired, angry, or perhaps all three.)

2. Ask the "white" person to whom Mrs. Parks should have given her seat: "How did you feel when Mrs. Parks refused to give you her seat?" (Angry that she wouldn't do what she was supposed to do.)

3. Ask the person who played the bus driver: "How did you feel when Rosa Parks refused to get up and you decided to call the police?" (Angry, that she wouldn't do what she was supposed to do; a little sad, perhaps, that you had to get someone else in trouble; perhaps a little of both.)

4. Ask the "police": "How did you feel when you had to take Mrs. Parks off the bus?" (Angry, that she wouldn't do what she was supposed to; the same as you usually feel—you were just doing the job you get paid to do.)

5. Ask the youths who played the "blacks": "Would you like being made to sit in the back of the bus all the time even though white people could sit wherever they wanted to?" (Some may say that they always choose to sit in the back. Try to stress the fact that this was not a choice; this would be something that they would have to do.) "Would you have liked to have to give up your seat whenever all the seats were filled and a white person got on the bus?" (No.) "How would you have felt as a black person when you heard that Rosa Parks had refused to give her bus seat to a white person?" (Happy; perhaps a little afraid of what might happen to her or to other blacks.)

6. Ask those who played the "whites": "If all your life you had been told that black people were supposed to sit in the back of the bus and get up to give white people their seats, how would you feel when you heard that Mrs. Parks had refused to give up her seat?" (Angry that she wouldn't do what she was supposed to do.)

Explain that it isn't likely that the whites would think that it was unfair or unjust for blacks to have to give up their seats. The whites would just think that that was the way it was supposed to be. Explain, also, that white people owned the bus company and that white people held the jobs as city officials who controlled what went on in the city.

7. Then ask the entire group: "If the white people were angry and thought that Mrs. Parks should have given up her seat, do you think that they would be willing to change things so that black people didn't have to give up their seats for whites anymore?" (No.)

8. "How do you think the black people's refusal to ride the buses helped change things?" (If the bus company did not have enough money, it couldn't run. Black people showed the bus company that it needed the bus fares black people paid in order to run the company and make money. The only way that the bus company would get bus fares from black people, though, would be if the company was willing to change things.)

"Martin Luther King, Jr., saw nonviolent confrontation as a way of practicing Christian love while fighting for justice. He taught black people simply to refuse to obey unfair laws and customs and helped them see that the force of love, and not the force of hatred and violence and fighting, would achieve justice. He knew that segregation had to be fought because as long as it was legal, both blacks and whites would think that black people are inferior to whites. King did not want people to believe that because it is not true.

"In 1960 some black students in America sat down at a lunch counter which was supposed to be used only by white people. The waitress refused to serve them any food, but King and his supporters and students all over the U.S. began to use 'sit-ins' as a nonviolent means of protest. Many blacks were jailed for protesting the unjust segregation laws. Others were beaten, bitten by police dogs, and even killed. They suffered greatly. As the country became more aware of the conditions that black people faced with unjust laws, some white Americans joined the protest.

"There were four steps to the nonviolent campaign which King proposed. First, facts were collected to show that injustice existed. Second, talks were attempted to solve the problem. Third, meetings were called to get volunteers. The volunteers were put through a program which would help them learn how not to fight back when they were attacked and how to love those who attacked them. Then the campaign moved to the fourth step: direct action. Direct action involved a boycott or sit-in at segregated or all-white lunch counters, at city libraries, or a kneel-in at white churches. Some volunteers marched to protest unfair laws."

Now read or have someone read the second role play.

Role Play #2

Jimmy Lee Jones is a black college student. He has seen the student sit-ins on TV. Several black students had sat down at a lunch counter that served only white people and asked for food. Instead of being served, they were arrested and taken to jail. Now Jimmy Lee and several of his friends are walking down to the five-

and-ten-cent store to participate in a sit-in. They know that some black students had been slapped and spit upon and cursed by white hecklers as they sat at the counter. They did not know what was going to happen to them, but they knew they had to go anyway.

Rearrange the chairs in front of a table as though they are seats at a lunch counter. Have some of the youth take the part of the black students and come in and sit down at the counter. Choose a waitress and store manager. Have several people act as white hecklers who harass and abuse the demonstrators. At the end of the role play, the police arrest the demonstrators and carry them out of the store. Have the members of the group make up the dialogue.

Discussion

1. "If the black people knew that they would not be served, why did they sit down at the counter?" (So that people everywhere would get to know how blacks were treated and begin to think about the unjust segregation laws and change them.)

2. Ask the "white" people who heckled the demonstrators: "If you had really been a white person there that day, how would you have felt seeing black people sitting at a counter that you knew had always been only for whites?" (Angry because "they" were trying to be where they weren't supposed to be.)

3. Ask the "waitress" and "manager": "If you had really been the waitress and manager there that day, how do you think you would have felt when the demonstrators refused to leave?" (Angry that they were making so much trouble for you or, perhaps, sad that you were going to get them into trouble.)

4. Ask the "police": "If you had really been the police there that day, how would you have felt?" (Perhaps angry because these people wouldn't do what they were supposed to do.)

5. Ask the "demonstrators": "If you had really been the demonstrators, how would you have felt when you sat down at the lunch counter?" (Scared, maybe, because you didn't want to go to jail.) "How did you feel when people began to heckle you?" (Sad and/or angry.)

Step 2—"He Was Oppressed and He Was Afflicted"

Read or tell the following summary of biblical background to the group:

We have seen that black people in the United States have often experienced much suffering and abuse. Suffering and abuse are not easy to put up with, but it is often out of suffering, abuse, and pain that God brings about great good.

Writing in the Book of Isaiah long before the birth of Jesus, a prophet told of One chosen by God whose unjust suffering would bring about a new kind of life (see especially Isaiah 42:1-4; 52:13–53:12). Jesus Christ is that chosen One. He was beaten and spat upon, condemned and killed unjustly although he did only good things, teaching the poor and healing the sick. In his life he showed us how to love as God loves. It was his mission to inaugurate the kind of world God wants, a world filled with justice, peace, love in the form of respect and compassionate concern, and well-being for all. Now, after his resurrection, Christ's Spirit guides his followers to continue his mission by living their lives as he lived his.

In the United States blacks have often been forced to live out the same suffering which Jesus Christ endured. And just as his suffering was transformed to bring about good, the suffering which blacks have experienced can, if we allow it, be transformed by Christ to bring about good. People who have suffered, who have been treated without respect and without compassion, often can come to realize more easily than those who have not been so treated how important these things are in human life. Because we have suffered, we have, in a very real sense, been especially chosen to live out the "Christ-life" of respect and compassionate concern for others, especially for those who are suffering as we have suffered. Unfortunately, experiences of suffering and abuse often bring other things besides compassion and understanding. People who have been forced to suffer often remain resentful and bitter or continue to feel worthless. Certainly, it is normal to have these feelings when one has been abused or caused to suffer. But when these feelings remain very intense, it is impossible for one to react with concern and understanding when others are suffering. It is these feelings which must be transformed by Christ if we are to carry out the mission for which he has chosen us.

Step 3—Prayer: "And with His Stripes We Are Healed"

Wait for silence. Then have the members of the group picture themselves in the presence of Christ. (Pause) Ask them to recall and picture before Christ one of the role plays in Step 1 in which they identified strongly with the people who suffered, or an instance of suffering from their own personal experience. (Pause) Have them experience again the feelings they had during the role play or personal experience they are picturing. (Pause) Encourage them to talk in their minds with Christ about the feelings. Since he went through great suffering, he can understand exactly what they feel. (Pause) Have them imagine what the feeling (anger, resentment, worthlessness, whatever) would look like. Have them hand an image of this feeling to Christ, and then watch to see what he will do with it. (Pause) Does he change it? If so, in what way is it changed? (Pause) Have the youth ask Christ how and with which person or persons they can now use this experience with suffering and what they learned from it. (Long pause) Allow those who wish to share their prayer experience with the group to do so.

Step 4—Activity: "The Crippled Child"

"The Crippled Child" is a West African cantefable (tale with a song) which shows that West Africans, even before Christianity, understood that suffering can be transformed into good. After giving the following background concerning the Yoruba people, whose story it is, tell the tale, teach the song, and have the members of the group act out the story. In the song the person playing the crippled child sings the "leader" parts, and everyone sings the "chorus" parts.

The ancestors of the present-day black Americans lived in Africa. There are many different peoples living in Africa. The Yoruba are one of these peoples. They live in the western part of Nigeria.

The Yoruba love to tell stories and act them out. Many of their tales are cantefables, i.e., tales with songs in them. To understand "The Crippled Child," you should know something about Yoruba life.

The Yoruba have many kings who rule over small kingdoms made up of several towns and villages. The kings wear crowns with strings of beads down the front which cover their faces. During the last century, there were many wars between the various kingdoms, and it was common for people to leave the villages that had been attacked. Kings, however, are not generally chosen only by consulting the Babalawo, as is done in this story.

The Babalawo is the priest of Ifa, the god of fate, or chance. Traditionally, the Yoruba believed in many gods and went to the Babalawo to find out what they should do in any situation. Today, of course, many Yoruba are Christian or Moslem.

The Crippled Child

There was once a mother who had seven children. One of these children was crippled. The town where they lived was at war with another town, and the mother decided to leave. She took the six well children with her but left the crippled child because he could not travel very fast.

The crippled child was left alone, but he decided to leave, too. As he hurried to get away from the enemy, he sang a song (at the bottom of this page).

93

Finally, when he had reached a town far away from the war, he stopped to beg. The crippled child did not know it, but the king of this region had just died. The people were going to ask the Babalawo who should be their next king. The Babalawo told them to choose the crippled beggar who had just come into their town, and the people made the crippled child their king.

Time passed. One day there appeared before the king a woman and her six children. They had just recently come to beg in that town. The king immediately recognized his own mother and his brothers and sisters, but they did not recognize him. He decided to test his mother before he told her who he was.

"Hail, Your Majesty!" said the woman as she knelt to greet the king. Her daughters were kneeling behind her, and her sons were prostrate because that is the correct way to greet a Yoruba king.

"The king greets you," the king replied. "Have you never had any other children?" he asked.

"I have had only these six children, sir," she said.

"Tell the truth," the king commanded.

"I had seven children once," she said, after a pause. "One died."

"How did your child die?" the king asked.

"He had a fever," the woman replied. "He cried and I rocked him for days and days, but he died and I buried him."

"This woman is lying," the king said to his attendants. "Take her out and kill her."

"Wait," the woman cried, "I will tell the truth. I did have seven children. One was crippled. When our town was being attacked, I left the crippled child and ran away with the other six. I have not seen my child since then."

"I am that child," said the king.

The woman immediately began to cry and to beg for mercy. The king forgave her for what she had done, gave her a house, and sent food and clothing for her and for his brothers and sisters.

(Step 5—Evaluation)

To evaluate the session with the group, see the suggestions given in Appendix E.

Seeing Need

PURPOSE

To enable youth
- —to see Christ in suffering
- —to become more aware of and sensitive to the suffering which surrounds us
- —to develop supportive listening skills

OUTLINE OF SESSION

Step 1—"How Many Birds"
Step 2—We Saw Thee Sick and a Stranger
Step 3—Observe!
Step 4—Listen!
Step 5—Intercessory Prayer
Step 6—Activity: Making an Intercession Notebook
(Step 7—Evaluation)

This session involves a period of observation of a ghetto street scene. Have the youth meet at a place located near where they will carry out their observations, go through Steps 1 and 2, observe for a stated period of time, and then return to the meeting place to continue the session. Or if you plan to omit Step 1, give the youth instructions as to what and where they are to observe (see Step 3); have them do the observation, and then meet at a given time in a centrally located place to carry out Step 2 and the rest of the session.

Step 1—"How Many Birds"

Note: This step may be omitted for older age groups.
"How Many Birds" is a children's singing circle game from West Africa. It is used here for exactly the same purpose that it is used in West Africa: to improve observation and awareness.

1. Have the members of the group form a circle with one person, the leader, in the middle.

2. Practice the song on page 96 with the group, with the leader singing the parts marked "leader" and everyone else singing the chorus parts.

3. After they sing the song, have the youth try to play the game which goes with it. As the leader begins the song, the rest of the group dances single file clockwise around the circle in time with the music.

4. When the leader gets to "Sho, sho, sho,[1] come and fly down," those in the circle face the center.

5. As they answer "Sho," those in the circle and the leader all stop momentarily.

6. Twice, after the leader sings "Sho, sho, sho, come and fly down," the others answer "Sho" and stoop.

[1] Sho—pronounced "Show."

7. When the leader sings "Sho, sho, sho, come and fly down" for the third time, no one answers "Sho" or stoops. Anyone who does is out.

Comment that it is necessary to observe very carefully and to be fully aware in order to play the game "How Many Birds" successfully, and such awareness is exactly what is necessary for the rest of the session.

Step 2—We Saw Thee Sick and a Stranger

1. Have the youth read Matthew 25:31-40 and Galatians 6:2.

2. Explain that the purpose of this session is to help the group become fully aware of the suffering that goes on in their midst, to help them to see Christ in their suffering sisters and brothers, and to learn to minister to him by learning how to be better ministers to those who are suffering. Point out that there are many ways in which people suffer. Some suffer physical pain. There are also the blind and the crippled. Others are in need, hungry, lonely, or are in conflict with those around them.

Step 3—Observe!

1. Assign the places where the various youth are to observe (perhaps in groups of two or three) and a time when they are to return.

2. Ask them to zero in on one or two people in the locale who seem to be unhappy or suffering in some way (from pain, hunger, loneliness, rejection, conflict with others, etc.) and try to imagine how those persons feel.

3. Send the group out to observe.

Step 4—Listen!

When the group returns, summarize the following comments for them: There are many times when we see people experiencing some kind of suffering and are not able to do anything to help them. However, there are also times when others ask us to listen as they tell us about what hurts them. At times such as these, there are several things that we can say to help the person who is talking feel more comfortable and know that he or she is understood or accepted. The most important thing, of course, is to listen attentively. It is also often helpful to a person in distress when you show that you understand what he or she has experienced through comments such as "I know how you felt." Summarizing what you think the other person has told you, or asking for clarification when you are not sure that you understand what he or she has said not only helps you get a clear picture of what is going on, but it also assures the person that you are listening sympathetically and helps him or her also to clarify the problem.

Shortly, you are going to share with one another in groups of twos the experience of one of the people whom you observed. As your partner does the talking, try to listen attentively and make occasional comments which show that you understand what he or she is saying. Ask for clarification when you don't understand, and when your partner has finished, try to summarize for him or her what you think was said. Try especially to respond to the feeling of pain, anger, frustration, or whatever the other person is trying to get across, as well as to the words.

1. Have the group divide into twos. Try to pair off people who observed in different locales.

2. While one partner attempts to use the listening skills just described, have the other member of the pair describe his or her observation in the following way:

(a) Imagine that you are actually the person you observed most closely.

(b) Describe the locale where you are, your appearance, and the situation in which you find yourself.

(c) Describe your condition and how you feel and how you react to persons and events around you.

3. After one member of the pair has had sufficient time to share his or her experience, ask everyone to change roles so that the listener now describes his or her experience in the same way and the partner who has shared becomes the attentive listener.

Step 5—Intercessory Prayer

After each partner has had an opportunity to share and to listen, ask the group to form a circle. Ask each youth in turn to offer a short description of the person described to him or her during Step 4, ending with a prayer for that person. End with a prayer for all those suffering in any way.

How Many Birds

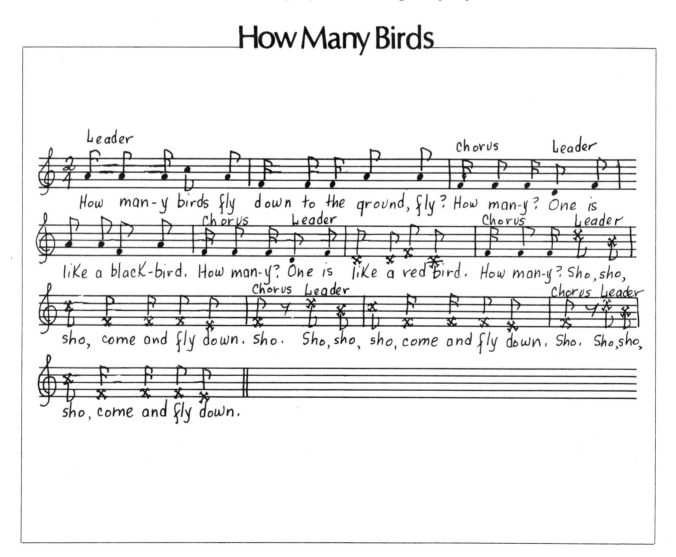

Step 6—Activity: Making an Intercession Notebook

1. Give each person a small notebook and pencil.

2. Tell the group that these notebooks are to be used to list names and/or descriptions of people for whom they wish to pray. They may also wish to list in this notebook names of those with whom they would like to try using their listening skills.

3. Ask the youth to jot down now in the notebook reminders to pray for those whom they have observed or whose story they have heard, as well as the names of family members, friends, and acquaintances for whom they wish to pray.

4. Ask them to keep the notebooks and to add to them from time to time.

(Step 7—Evaluation)

To evaluate the session with the group, see the suggestions given in Appendix E.

A Long-Term Project: Doing Something About Suffering

God's Revelation: ". . . . In the world ye shall have tribulation: but be of good cheer; I have overcome the world" (John 16:33). "Bear ye one another's burdens . . ." (Galatians 6:2).

Our Response: Where do I see suffering and tribulation? How do I allow Christ to overcome/transform suffering for me and, through me, for others?

The long-term project for this unit can cover at least nine meetings, in addition to the time set aside for religious celebration, if all the above outlined sessions are used. An outline for the nine meetings is given below. The mid-project revision and any of the outlined sessions in the unit can, of course, be omitted.

SAMPLE OUTLINE

Meeting 1—Commitment Service (see Appendix F) and Session I

Meeting 2—Session III

Meeting 3—Session II

Meeting 4—Session IV

Meeting 5—Plan the social action project

Meeting 6—Discuss ways to cope with negative aspects of the social action project; plan home devotions

Meeting 7—Plan and prepare for a religious celebration on the theme
—Celebration

Meeting 8—Mid-project revision

Meeting 9—Evaluation

A RETREAT ON SUFFERING, ELECTION, AND MISSION

A retreat can be planned on this theme using the suggested outline given in Appendix M. Session IV can be adapted for a retreat by using a film, slide show, or set of mounted pictures. A set of such pictures, entitled "Value of Life," is available from the Seabury Bookstore, 815 Second Avenue, New York, NY 10017 for $5.00. Ask the youth to imagine how the people shown in these pictures feel.

SOCIAL ACTION PROJECT SUGGESTIONS

There are several different projects which the group might undertake on this theme. In one project the members of the group might volunteer as visitors or aides at a local nursing home, home for the elderly, or hospital. There the listening skills described in Session IV could be used to help those who may be suffering. Another project might involve a presentation by the group of the history of blacks in this country. The presentation might illustrate (1) how the suffering which has been a part of black history can provide a basis for understanding and helping those who are experiencing suffering now or (2) how the struggle for freedom, justice, and human dignity, which has been a part of that history, must continue as part of a mission to help all people obtain these human rights.

SOME SUGGESTIONS FOR RESEARCHING THE PROJECTS
For Volunteer Visitors or Aides

• Contact local nursing homes, homes for the elderly, and/or hospitals to determine whether or not they have volunteer visitors or aides, whether or not they give training programs for volunteers, age requirements, etc.

• Set up role plays, or practice duos (as in Session IV, Step 4) based on common experiences and situations in nursing homes, homes for the elderly, or hospitals.

• Ask a hospital or nursing home chaplain or your minister for help in developing listening skills.

For a Black History Presentation

Information concerning the history of black people in the United States can be obtained from John Hope Franklin's book *From Slavery to Freedom* (3rd edition) (New York: Alfred A. Knopf, Inc., 1967) or *Before the Mayflower: A History of the Negro in America, 1619–1964* by Lerone Bennett, Jr. (Baltimore: Penguin Books, 1966) or some other standard black history text.

COPING WITH NEGATIVE ASPECTS

Conflicts can occur in dealing with persons confined to nursing homes, homes for the elderly, or hospitals. Attempting to empathize with the person involved (as in Session II, Step 3) is very important. Setting up role plays based on the conflict situations, following them with discussions of the feelings involved, and having frank discussions of the difficult situations with the entire group during mid-project revision may prove helpful. For additional suggestions on coping with negative aspects of the social action project, see Appendix H.

HOME DEVOTIONS

In addition to the biblical passages and meditations given in the outlined sessions, the following Bible passages may be useful for home devotions: Psalms 22; 40; 69:1-21; Matthew 26:36–28:10; Mark 14:32–16:11; Luke 22:39–24:12; John 18:1–20:18; 2 Timothy 2:11-12a. Collects and prayers from *The Book of Common Prayer* which are appropriate for this theme include the collects for Palm Sunday (p. 219), Monday in Holy Week (p. 220), Holy Saturday (p. 221), the Third Sunday in Easter (p. 224), the Annunciation (p. 240), for Social Service (p. 260), and prayers for the poor and neglected (#35, p. 826) and for the sick (pp. 458-460). For additional suggestions concerning home devotions, see Appendix I.

CELEBRATION

The celebration of the Eucharist, or Holy Communion, is obviously intimately connected to the theme of suffering, election, and mission. In this service Christ's suffering and death are transformed to become a source of life for us. Our suffering and struggle, offered in union with his in this celebration, can be transformed by Christ and used by him to become a source of healing and renewal for others. For general comments on using the Eucharist for the celebration, see Appendix J.

MUSIC

"There Is a Balm in Gilead," "God Will Take Care of You," "Come to Me," "Didn't My Lord Deliver Daniel?" "Were You There?," "I Must Tell Jesus," "Take My Hand, Precious Lord," and "Nobody Knows the Trouble I've Seen" are all hymns which would be appropriate for this theme.

EVALUATION

See "Suggestions for Project Evaluation," Appendix L.

Unit on Bread

Background

7

Jesus is the bread of life, and it is in his life that we find life spiritually. However, in the Gospels we see evidence that Christ—that God—is concerned about more than just the spiritual well-being of his people. Jesus feeds the multitude and teaches his disciples to pray, "Give us this day our daily bread." God is concerned that we have what is necessary to give us life and strength physically and emotionally, as well as spiritually.

For many black youth in America today it has become increasingly difficult to find jobs to earn "bread," that is, money, to live. Many families in this country go hungry in the midst of plenty while estimates of the absolute poor or malnourished in parts of Africa and in some other places in the developing world range as high as 80 or 90 percent.

It is important that the church, the body of Christ, show the same concern for the physical, emotional, and spiritual well-being of God's people as was shown by Jesus Christ, our Head. The sessions in this unit are designed to provide opportunities for the youth to examine the problem of teenage unemployment and, in the suggested projects, to study the question of hunger both nationally and internationally. Sessions and suggested projects also provide opportunities to take some action locally with regard to these problems.

Help Wanted

PURPOSE

To enable youth
—to see that Christ is concerned that we have the necessities of life physically, emotionally, and spiritually
—to discover how few job opportunities are available for high school students, dropouts, and graduates without further training
—to experience the frustrations of being unable to find work
—to take some action to support one another and others who are unable to find jobs

OUTLINE OF SESSION

Step 1—Want Ads
Step 2—Jesus, the Bread of Life
Step 3—Prayer: "When Saw We Thee an Hungred?"
Step 4—Activity: "Help Wanted" Board
(Step 5—Evaluation)

Step 1—Want Ads

1. Furnish each member of the group with the "Help Wanted" section of a current newspaper and scissors.

2. Have each person cut out any job listings for which a high school dropout or graduate without further training could apply.

3. Have the members of the group count the total number of suitable ads which they were able to find. Then put the clippings in a safe place for use in Step 4 (Help Wanted Board).

4. Comment: "The unemployment rate for black youth in the U.S. is running about 38 percent per month, according to government statistics. That means that out of every ten black youth who are looking for jobs, only about six will find work. The ads which we have just cut out of the paper would probably not provide enough jobs for all the local black youth who are looking for work. Today we are going to explore how it feels to be looking for a job and unable to find one."

5. Divide the group into two groups for a role play. Members of one group will play high school dropouts looking for work. The other group members will play the part of prospective employers. Each group will advise its players as to how to play the parts. (Any youth with actual experience in unsuccessful job seeking can provide advice from his or her personal experience.)

6. Have the players create the action and dialogue for each situation below.

7. Stop at the stopping points suggested, and ask the job seeker and his or her group what they think the job seeker's feelings would be at that point.

Situation #1: A black teenager in his or her first attempt to find a job.

Possible Stopping Points:
- The youth walks into an employment office filled with other job seekers.
- The interviewer asks the job seeker what work experience he or she has had; he or she has had none.
- The job seeker is given confusing instructions for filling in an application form and is told that there really aren't very many openings at this time.

8. Have the groups switch roles. The group members that have portrayed prospective employers now play the part of job seekers who have graduated from high school but who have no other special training. The group members that were job seekers now portray prospective employers.

Situation #2: A black high school graduate who has been looking for work for a month and has already tried unsuccessfully at three other places that day.

Possible Stopping Points:
- There is a long wait before the applicant can see the interviewer, even though there aren't many other job seekers in the office.
- The applicant is told to go to another office where they may be hiring.
- The office to which he or she has been referred is closed for the day.

It is probable that the youth will express feelings of frustration, anger, discouragement, confusion, worthlessness, disgust, and desperation at the various stopping points.

Step 2—Jesus, the Bread of Life

Read or have the members of the group read Matthew 4:4; John 6:35; Matthew 6:11; John 6:5-14; Mark 6:31-44; and Matthew 25:34-40. Then summarize the comments below on the passages.

We know that Jesus Christ is the bread of life, that his Spirit feeds us spiritually and strengthens us to live a life like his life in our world. But we see that Jesus was concerned not only with people's spiritual welfare, but he also gave actual bread to those who were hungry and taught us to ask God in prayer for the food which we need to eat daily in order to live. Furthermore, he showed us that in feeding the hungry, we are serving him, feeding him.

There are many different ways in which people hunger in our world. Some people are actually physically hungry. They need to be given free food and/or a job or a lead to a job in order to make money to buy food. Some of those who have spent months unsuccessfully searching for a job also are emotionally hungry for signs of concern and encouragement from those around them. We have just seen how frustrating and discouraging job hunting can be. How can we feed the Christ in one another and in friends and acquaintances who have tried again and again unsuccessfully to get work?

Step 3—Prayer: "When Saw We Thee an Hungred?"

1. Ask the group to sit in silence for a short while.
2. Then ask each member of the group to imagine that he or she is bringing into the presence of Christ someone who is physically, emotionally, or spiritually hungry, or who has been searching unsuccessfully for a job for a long time. The person brought can be the group member himself or herself, a family member, friend, or acquaintance, or someone unknown. (Pause)
3. Ask the members of the group to picture themselves introducing the person to Christ and telling

him something of how the person feels. (Pause)
4. Have the group members step back for a while to watch while Christ ministers to the person they have brought. (Pause)
5. Have the members of the group ask Christ to show them in what way they can minister to the hunger in the person they have brought and thus feed Christ in feeding him or her. (Pause)
6. Allow all who wish to share their prayer experience with the group to do so.

Step 4—Activity: "Help Wanted" Board

Have the members of the group jointly make a "Help Wanted" board to be placed somewhere in the church building for members of the congregation to post odd-job notices. With crayons, paints, construction paper, or magazine pictures, the youth can decorate the board attractively. Post on it at this session those want ads which the group thinks might be suitable (see Step 1) as well as Bible passages and the group's own short statements concerning Christ's concern for our physical, emotional, and spiritual needs. Be sure to have someone from the group encourage the congregation to make use of the board.

(Step 5—Evaluation)

To evaluate the session with members of the group, see the suggestions given in Appendix E.

Canvass

PURPOSE

To enable youth

—to see that Christ is concerned that we have the necessities of life emotionally, physically, and spiritually

—to discover some likely places of employment for high school dropouts and graduates

—to do something positive for unemployed youth in the area

OUTLINE OF SESSION

BEFORE THE CANVASS

Step 1—"He . . . blessed, and brake the loaves"

Step 2—Prayer: Bread

Step 3—Canvass Preparation

AFTER THE CANVASS

Step 4—Report

Step 5—Activity: Help Wanted Newssheet

(Step 6—Evaluation)

This session involves a canvass for which some advance preparation is necessary. In advance, decide on a central location where the youth will meet before the event to prepare for canvassing and afterward to report on their findings. Local fast-food outlets (for example, Gino's), supermarkets and other grocery stores, movie houses, offices that use messengers, and other businesses with a high turnover in personnel can be canvassed by the youth for possible job openings and information on how to apply for a job. Decide before the event whether the youth will canvass singly or in groups of two or more, who will go to which places, how long the actual canvassing should take, when the canvassers will report back on their findings, etc. A form such as the following one can be mimeographed in advance and given to the canvassers to remind them of the necessary questions to ask.

Suggested Questions for Canvassers

1. What kinds of jobs are available for high school youth without any special training?

2. Where does one apply for a job? In the case of chain supermarkets or fast-food outlets (for example, Gino's), does one apply at a central office or at individual locations?

3. To whom should one apply for a job?

4. Is there an age limit (for example, over eighteen)?

5. What are the skills necessary (for example, the ability to count change)?

6. What are the hours?

7. Is part-time employment available?

8. What is the salary (for each kind of job)?

9. How does one apply for a job? By written application? By interview?

10. Does the applicant have to bring any documents (for example, a Social Security card)?

BEFORE THE CANVASS: Step 1—"He . . . blessed, and brake the loaves"

To begin the session, comment on the extremely high unemployment rate among black youth and introduce the canvass which the group is going to undertake. As a biblical and theological background for the session, use the Bible passages and summary given in "Jesus, the Bread of Life," Session I, Step 2.

BEFORE THE CANVASS: Step 2—Prayer: Bread

You may want to use as a focal point for this prayer an actual loaf of bread placed on a table in the center of the group. Wait for silence, then ask the members of the group to imagine themselves in the presence of Christ. Have them "free-associate," that is, see what ideas come to mind in connection with the word "bread" and what they have just heard in the Bible passages and summary. As the Spirit moves them, ask them to speak what comes to their minds. End with a short prayer asking God's blessing on the canvass to be undertaken.

BEFORE THE CANVASS: Step 3—Canvass Preparation

Give all necessary information for carrying out the operation successfully (assign locations to be canvassed, hand out question sheets, etc.), and be sure to agree on a time for everyone to return and continue the session. (If you wish, the actual canvass and the continuation of the session can take place on another day.)

AFTER THE CANVASS: Step 4—Report

Have the canvassers report their findings. You may want to have the youth use the completed question sheets to set up a card file where all the information concerning possible job openings and how one applies for them will be readily available.

AFTER THE CANVASS: Step 5—Activity: Help Wanted Newssheet

Have the members of the group put together a rough

draft of a Help Wanted newssheet. Along with any job opportunities discovered during the canvass and the information necessary for applying for them, the newssheet can include artwork, Bible verses, some of the youth's statements during the prayer in Step 2 above, or other statements concerning Christ's concern for our emotional, spiritual, and physical needs. Have the newssheet mimeographed and posted or distributed at places where youth congregate.

(Step 6—Evaluation)

To evaluate the session with members of the group, see the suggestions given in Appendix E.

A Long-Term Project: Doing Something About Teenage Unemployment or Hunger

God's Revelation: "Inasmuch as ye have done it unto one of the least of these my brethren, ye have done it unto me" (Matthew 25:40).

Our Response: How can we go about feeding Christ in our brothers and sisters today?

The long-term project for this unit can be accomplished in as few as five meetings or as many as seven meetings, in addition to the religious celebration. Seven meetings would include both Sessions I and II above as well as a mid-project revision meeting. An outline for this plan follows. To finish the project in five meetings, omit either Session I or Session II and the mid-project revision meeting.

SAMPLE OUTLINE

Meeting 1—Commitment Service (see sample in Appendix F) and either Session I or II

Meeting 2—Either Session I or II (whichever was not used for the first meeting)

Meeting 3—Plan the social action project

Meeting 4—Discuss ways to cope with negative aspects of the social action project; plan home devotions

Meeting 5—Plan and prepare for a religious celebration on the theme
—Celebration

Meeting 6—Mid-project revision

Meeting 7—Evaluation

SOCIAL ACTION PROJECT SUGGESTIONS
On Teenage Unemployment

Plan and run a workshop for local youth on what is involved in applying and interviewing for a job.

On Local or World Hunger

• Make available for the church office a list of local feeding programs, i.e., their location and information concerning eligibility; make available information concerning eligibility for food stamps and where and how they can be obtained.

• Present a program to publicize the facts concerning world hunger and particularly concerning hunger in Africa and in other parts of the Third World.

SOME SUGGESTIONS FOR RESEARCHING THE PROJECTS
For a Workshop on Applying and Interviewing for a Job

• Contact a counselor from the state employment agency or another employment agency for advice.

• With the help of a job counselor collect job application forms and practice filling them in properly.

• With the help of a job counselor, practice interviewing for a job.

• Investigate what documents are generally needed for getting a job (for example, Social Security card) and how to go about securing them.

• If possible, obtain from a job counselor a list of the kinds of jobs available for high school students, dropouts, and graduates; what skills are necessary for the jobs; etc. (See Session II, Suggested Questions for Canvassers.)

Making Available Information on Feeding Programs and Food Stamps

• Throughout the U.S. many different feeding programs are available. Some of these include Meals on Wheels or are available through day care centers, soup kitchens, school lunch programs, senior citizen nutrition centers, and school breakfast programs. Church food pantries also provide supplementary canned goods and other staples. To determine which of these programs is available in your community, contact your local or regional denominational headquarters, the Salvation Army, and the county welfare department. (In contacting the county welfare department, look in the white pages of the telephone book under County Government for a title such as Office of Health and Welfare, or Health and Social Services, or Health and Social Welfare—different counties use different titles.)

• Inquire about information concerning the Food Stamp program (eligibility, how one applies, where available, etc.) through the county welfare office which has responsibility for health and welfare or social services (see above).

• Send for information on hunger from your national denominational headquarters, or subscribe to *Hunger Notes* from World Hunger Education Service, 200 P Street, NW, Washington, DC 20036. The Episcopal Church publishes its own edition of *Hunger Notes* which is available free of charge to Episcopalians from the Reverend Charles Cesaretti, Episcopal Church Center, 815 Second Avenue, New York, NY 10017.

For Presenting a Program to Publicize World Hunger

Hunger Notes (see above) includes extensive bibliographies and audiovisual resource guides as well as specific articles and suggestions for planning programs and local projects and for getting involved in ongoing national projects concerning local and world hunger.

COPING WITH NEGATIVE ASPECTS

Certain tasks necessary for carrying out any of these projects successfully (for example, locating a job counselor or other qualified, interested adult to assist with the job workshop; tracking down information concerning feeding programs and food stamps) require patience and persistence and can be frustrating and discouraging. Youth chosen to carry out these tasks may need generous support from the group and a frank appraisal of what is or is not possible in their particular circumstances. (It may not be possible, for example, to obtain actual job application forms for use in the job workshop. However, it may be possible to make up a form which includes many of the questions which usually crop up on application forms.) See also Appendix H, "Coping with Negative Aspects in a Social Action Project," for additional general suggestions.

HOME DEVOTIONS

For a general form for use in home devotions, see Appendix I. Bible passages and commentaries and prayers given in the outlines above (see Session I, Steps 2 and 3, and Session II, Steps 1 and 2) can all be made a part of home devotions. In addition, these Bible passages can be used: Deuteronomy 14:28-29; 24:19-22; Psalm 82:3-4; Isaiah 58:6-9; Luke 3:9-11; 2 Corinthians 8:8-15; James 2:14-17. Appropriate prayers for this theme from *The Book of Common Prayer* are numbers 30, 29, and 35 on pages 824 and 826.

CELEBRATION

If a Eucharist or Holy Communion is used for the religious celebration which is part of the long-term project, the first part of the service on pages 400ff. in *The Book of Common Prayer* can be used and can include some of the Bible passages, prayer, study, and discussion which have already taken place in the unit. An appropriate Gospel passage for this celebration would be John 6:48-69. An explanation such as the following could also be summarized and given, adapted for your particular group.

In the Eucharist, Christ comes to us in a special way. Just as bread feeds us physically and enables us to live and grow, in the Eucharist Christ himself, the Word of God, is the bread who feeds us spiritually and enables us to live and grow as vital parts of his Body here on earth. As we live and grow in Christ, we begin to actualize in our own lives the total faith in God and obedience to God's will and the concern and compassion for others which we see in Christ's life. In Christ's life we see concern and compassion for the total well-being of those with whom he came in contact. We see him feeding those who hunger for actual food as well as those who hunger spiritually. In our world today there are many who are hungry, who are without jobs and unable to buy food, who have become discouraged in the struggle for survival. As parts of his Body, we offer our service to them in union with the sacrifice Christ made on Calvary, which is re-presented before us in the Eucharist. And as he comes to us in the service, he strengthens and empowers us, as part of his Body, to go forth and carry out this service in his name.

For general information concerning the Eucharist and suggestions for planning it, see Appendix J.

MUSIC

Music appropriate for this unit might include "Let Us Break Bread Together on Our Knees," "Break Thou the Bread of Life," "I've Just Come from the Fountain," "I'm A-Going to Eat at the Welcome Table," or any of the hymns in the "Holy Communion" section of *The Hymnal, 1940* (numbers 189-213).

EVALUATION

See "Suggestions for Project Evaluation," Appendix L.

Unit on Loving Ourselves

Background

8

In the summary of the law our Lord tells us, "Love the Lord your God with all your heart, . . . soul, and . . . mind. . . . And . . . your neighbor as yourself" (Matthew 22:37, 39). We often find it difficult to love neighbor as we love self not so much because we don't try to keep the commandment but because we do not really love the self that we truly are. Unconsciously we may refuse to accept the self that we are and end up spending a lot of time trying to prove to ourselves and to others that that self is really good enough to be loved and admired. We may fear, for example, that we are not really intelligent or beautiful or handsome and as a result of that fear spend so much time trying to show others that we are, indeed, intelligent or beautiful or handsome that we are left with little time to think of our neighbor.

Worse yet, we often end up trying to aggrandize ourselves at the expense of others. Much of the "put-down" humor, especially popular with black youth ("playing the dozens," "scoring," etc.) is used to do just this. It is, perhaps, especially popular with teens and preteens because boys and girls at this stage in their lives are still trying to carve out for themselves an identity that is valued by society. And as blacks we may frequently use this device because for so many years the general society insisted that black people's intelligence, physical characteristics, etc., were inferior to those of whites.

This unit is designed to help the youth in your group, first, become aware of what is really taking place in the "put-down" humor which they use and which is also used in some television programs. Then the sessions give the youth an opportunity to affirm themselves and one another. By affirming themselves and by being affirmed by one another, the members of the group can come to see themselves as acceptable and lovable. This will enable them both to love and accept themselves and eventually to love others more freely because they no longer find it necessary to prove themselves at the expense of others.

Lower Your Mask, Please

PURPOSE

To enable youth
  —to become aware of what lies behind much of the "put-down" humor they use
  —to be able to substitute affirming responses for "put-downs"
  —to "recycle" previous responses

OUTLINE OF SESSION

  Step 1—Masks
  Step 2—Which Mask Am I Wearing?
  Step 3—Love Self, Love Others
  Step 4—Back-Pedaling to Go Forward
  (Step 5—Evaluation)

Some caution should be exercised in leading this session. Read through the entire session carefully. In choosing persons for the skits in Step 2, be sure that no one is put in a position where he or she actually feels put down or laughed at. In other words, be careful *not* to choose someone who might think that he or she is ugly or someone who is fat for Skit I; or someone who is poorer than the rest of the group for Skit II; or someone who is weak for Skit III; or persons who are skinny or short for Skit IV; or people who seem less intelligent than the rest of the group for Skit V; or someone whose clothes would be commented on unfavorably for Skit VI.

After reading through the skits in Step 2 and deciding which ones you will use with the group, determine how many and which types of masks you will need to have the group make. For example, if you decide to use Skits I and III, your group will have to make at least one "handsome" mask (to show that each of the persons portrayed in these skits is trying to project himself or herself as handsome at the expense of the other). You can, of course, make up additional skits to use in Step 2. Be sure, however, to have the group make additional masks, if necessary, in Step 1 to go with the new skits.

Step 1—Masks

Divide the youth into groups and have them make hand-held masks to be used in Step 2. The masks are to portray the way in which the "put-downer" is trying to seem better than his or her "victim." Do not, however, tell the group members at this point why they are making the masks. Masks can be made from cardboard and decorated with paint, crayons, sequins, etc., to indicate what they portray. (For example, a

"wealthy" mask might be decorated with dollar signs.) If attached at the bottom to a stick, the mask can be held in front of the face.

Step 2—Which Mask Am I Wearing?

1. Assign youth to act out the skits below.

2. Before each group of two acts out the skit assigned to them, have the "put-downer" select a mask which will portray in which way he or she is pretending to be better than the person being put down. (For example, the second person in Skit II is trying to show that he or she is wealthier than the first person. In some skits—Skits I, IV, and V—both youth will have to use a mask since each is trying to be better than the other in some way.)

3. Have each duo act out the skit assigned to it. As the "put-downer" gives the "victim" the lines, have him or her hold the mask in front of his or her face.

4. Ask the person who is put down to explain how he or she feels as a result of what was said.

5. Have the entire group make suggestions to the person who played the "put-downer" of what could be substituted for the put-down in the skit situation—i.e., what would affirm the other person and make him or her feel good.

Skit I

1ST PERSON: Hey, how you doing? Hey, why do you fix your hair like that? You think it makes you look handsome (beautiful)? Look, you are so ugly that when you were born, the doctor slapped the wrong end.

2ND PERSON: That's all right. At least, I'm not fat. You're so fat that when you sit around the house, you really sit *around* the house.

Skit II

1ST PERSON: Hey, lend me a dime.

2ND PERSON: You mean you haven't got any money again? Honestly, you are so poor that if you decided to move in with the cats and dogs, you couldn't afford it.

Skit III

(Two boys are carrying things. One has more than the other.)

PERSON WITH LARGER LOAD: Is that all you can carry? Man, you are *weak*. How are you ever going to take up for yourself? You are so weak that you couldn't even beat an ant with a broken leg.

Skit IV

(One person runs up and catches the other's arm.)
1ST PERSON: Hey, let go of my arm.
2ND PERSON: Oh, I thought it was a toothpick.
1ST PERSON: Well, I may be thin, but at least I'm not so low that I have to play handball with the curb.

Skit V

(In the middle of an ongoing conversation)
1ST PERSON: Why did you tell her that? You are so dumb that your only idea died of loneliness.
2ND PERSON; Well, at least I'm not as dumb as you are. You're so dumb you have to cut a hole in your umbrella just to see if it's raining.

Skit VI

(Two people meet.)
1ST PERSON: Where'd you get that dress (those pants)? Gee, you sure wear some funny-looking clothes. Your dad must be the leader of Trash Can Diggers, Incorporated.

Step 3—Love Self, Love Others

1. Have the youth turn to Matthew 22:39.
2. Summarize the following for the group:

"In order for us to love our neighbor properly, it is important that we love ourselves. That is, we must be able to love ourselves in the sense of being able to accept and feel comfortable with the self that we really are in order to love our neighbor properly. If, for example, I do not really feel comfortable with the way I look, then I may frequently try to prove to myself that I am more handsome or more beautiful than someone else, or at least not as ugly or as fat as another person.

In other words, I may try to make myself feel comfortable about how I look at someone else's expense. Only when I can accept and love and feel comfortable with the self I really am will I be able to stop worrying about myself and love others. Often, when the self that I really am is accepted and affirmed by others, I can eventually come to love and accept my true self. Let us try, as a beginning, to affirm one another in love so that we can each come to love and accept ourselves and thus be free to love our neighbor as we love ourselves."

Step 4—Back-Pedaling to Go Forward

1. Have the youth imagine that they are in the presence of Christ. (Pause)
2. Ask them to recall either (*a*) an event where they were the "put-downer" or (*b*) an event where they were put down by someone else. What were the feelings of the person who was put down? What were their feelings if they were the one being put down? If they were the "put-downer," in what way were they trying to prove themselves better than the other person? (Pause)
3. Ask the youth, if they pictured an event where they were the "put-downer," to ask Christ to forgive them for having hurt another person. Have them ask Christ to enable them to love and accept themselves and to make a commitment to ask forgiveness of the person they put down. (Pause)
4. If they were the one put down, have them imagine Christ healing their hurt or angry feelings so that they can freely forgive the person who put them down.

(Step 5—Evaluation)

To evaluate the session with the group, see the suggestions given in Appendix E.

"Scoring" in the Big Times

PURPOSE

To enable youth
—to become aware of what lies behind much of the put-down humor they use
—to be able to substitute affirming responses for put-downs

OUTLINE OF SESSION

Step 1—Viewing
Step 2—Discussing
Step 3—Somebody's Standing in Front of the Light
Step 4—I Like That
Step 5—Prayer
Step 6—Activity: Read the Tag
(Step 7—Evaluation)

Step 1—Viewing

Ask the group to watch (either singly or together) one of the TV programs which uses a lot of put-down humor. Ask each person to make a note of several of the jokes that are used.

Step 2—Discussing

At a meeting of the group held after the TV program, ask the youth to repeat some of the jokes used in the program. Have them distinguish between those jokes which were intended to put down another person and those which were funny for other reasons. In the case of the put-down humor, discuss how the person who was put down felt and what the person who did the putting down was trying to say about himself or herself or achieve for himself or herself. Use several examples.

Step 3—Somebody's Standing in Front of the Light

Have the members of the group use a small lamp and two or more mirrors to reflect the light from the lamp to different parts of the room and from one person to another. Have someone stand in front of the light to see whether or not any light can be reflected when that person is standing there. Have the youth read Matthew 5:16; 22:39; John 8:12; 10:30; 2 Corinthians 4:6; and 1 John 4:16. Explain that God is love, that we see that love in Jesus Christ, and that we are to reflect the love which we have seen in Jesus into the lives of those around us, as the mirrors have reflected the light from the lamp around the room. Often, however, something stands in front of the light, and it is impossible for the light to be reflected as it should be. When we cannot accept and love the self that we are, we often try to build ourselves up at the expense of others. We put ourselves in front of the light and put down others. In order to reflect God's love and to love our neighbor, we have to love and accept the self that we are so that we are not always trying to build ourselves up at others' expense.

Step 4—I Like That

Have each person take a piece of newsprint, write his or her name on it, and list some of the things that he or she likes about himself or herself. Put the sheets of newsprint on the wall, and have the youth go around the room adding to the lists what they like about the person whose name is at the top of the sheet. Have the group members sit where they can see all of the sheets, and go around the room reading each sheet and allowing each person to accept the good things which others have written about him or her.

Step 5—Prayer

Gather in a circle. Ask each person first to imagine that he or she is in the presence of Christ. Ask the members silently to confess to him those times when in humor or in other ways they have tried to put down others or build themselves up at others' expense. Then go around the circle, and, one at a time, have each one thank God for the person on his or her left and for one of his or her good characteristics. To conclude, ask them to pledge silently to try to uphold and affirm one another; then present this offering through Christ to God.

Step 6—Activity: Read the Tag

On adhesive-backed name tags, have each person make at least one decorative button about one or more of the good characteristics listed on his or her sheet of newsprint. Encourage the members of the group to wear their tags. Good "mood music" to play while making the tags might be "You Don't Have to Be a Star" or some other appropriate recording.

(Step 7—Evaluation)

To evaluate the session with members of the group, see the suggestions given in Appendix E.

Unit on Black Men, Black Women

Background

9

The relationship between black men and black women is sometimes described as difficult because, it is said, black women often take over the roles which black men should hold. Session I in this unit compares the roles played by some black women in the lives of their people with those played by some Israelite women. It considers these roles in the light of the biblical theme of God as the true Savior who often accomplishes the deliverance and survival of a people purposely through what seems the most improbable means.

As youth grow into adults, there is a need for a frank discussion of sex as a good gift of God and one, like God's other gifts, to be used appropriately. The second session in this unit is designed to facilitate this discussion. It also explores the problem of sexual abuse and exploitation and the biblical concept of the body as the temple of God.

The Weak Confound the Mighty

PURPOSE

To enable youth
- —to be acquainted with the lives of great women in the Bible and in black history
- —to see the role that these women played as necessary for the well-being of their people

OUTLINE OF SESSION

Step 1—MW, Mw, or mW?
Step 2—Name That Person
Step 3—"For Such a Time as This"
Step 4—Prayer: Litany
Step 5—Activity: Dramatize "Oluronbi"
(Step 6—Evaluation)

Step 1—MW, Mw, or mW?

1. Give each person a sheet of paper and a pencil.

2. Ask each person to number on the paper from 1 to 10.

3. Tell the group members that you will read to them a list of ten jobs or functions. If they believe that a job or function is more likely to be done by a man than by a woman, then they are to write a capital M and a small w (Mw) after its number. If it is more likely to be done by a woman than by a man, then write mW after its number. If a job is as likely to be done by a woman as by a man, then write MW after its number.

4. Read the list of jobs or functions below, and have the youth record their answers on their papers.
- Lead troops into battle
- Act as ambassador to a king or government
- Start a college
- Be a judge
- Be a lecturer
- Serve as a spy
- Make and sell pies
- Start a protest movement
- Act as breadwinner for the household
- Act as head of the house

5. Ask one person to serve as recorder. As each member of the group reads his or her answers, have the recorder mark how many Mws, mWs, and MWs answers there are for each job or function. Read the totals for each job.

Step 2—Name That Person

1. Write the following list of names on newsprint or on the board:
David

Paul
Esther
Frederick Douglass
Rosa Parks
W. E. B. Du Bois
Mary McLeod Bethune
Harriet Tubman
Marcus Garvey
Elijah
Deborah

2. Comment: "Here on the board (on the newsprint) is a list of famous men and women. Some of them are men and women who lived during biblical times, and some are blacks who lived during the last two hundred years. I am going to read you five sets of clues which describe five of the people on the list. Listen to the clues, and then pick from the list the name of the person whom the clues fit." Read the clue sets but be sure NOT to read the name of the famous person at the end of the clues.

Clue Set #1

- was an Israelite judge
- summoned an Israelite warrior, Barak, to raise an army to fight the Canaanites
- with Barak, led the Israelite army to victory against the Canaanite general, Sisera, and his nine hundred chariots

The famous person: Deborah

Clue Set #2

- a Jew living in Persia
- given a high position by the king of Persia
- at this time, Haman, the Persian prime minister, persuaded the king to issue a command to have all the Jews in Persia destroyed
- implored by Mordecai, a Jewish leader, to intercede with the king for the Jews
- saved the Jews from destruction by interceding with the king

The famous person: Esther

Clue Set #3

- born a slave in the United States
- escaped from slavery
- returned to the South approximately nineteen times to lead hundreds of other slaves to freedom
- called "Black Moses"
- acted as a spy for the Union Army in the Civil War

The famous person: Harriet Tubman

Clue Set #4

- born in South Carolina just after the Civil War
- worked as a child picking cotton in the fields
- studied at Scotia Seminary and Moody Bible Institute
- opened a college for blacks in Florida
- sold pies to obtain money for the college
- was asked by President Roosevelt to direct the National Youth Administration division for blacks, which provided emergency education for poor black youth in rural areas during the Depression
- organized the National Council of Negro Women

The famous person: Mary McLeod Bethune

Clue Set #5

- lived in Montgomery, Alabama
- made a living making clothing
- refused to stand on a Montgomery bus so that a white man could sit down, and was arrested
- sparked the civil rights movement of the 1950s and 1960s

The famous person: Rosa Parks

After all the famous people have been identified, comment: "We see that all the famous people in this exercise are women. One served as a judge and a leader in battle, one acted as ambassador on behalf of her people before the Persian king, one served as a spy, another founded a college, and the last sparked a protest movement. In other words, all of these women did things which we tend to associate more often with men than with women.

"In the black community, many people have expressed a concern that black women have often taken over the roles that black men should play. Black women in America have frequently served as heads of their households and breadwinners for their families, as well as, in exceptional cases, acting as spies, founding colleges, and sparking protest movements. The question which many ask is whether the strong and courageous role which black American women have played necessarily 'un-mans' and undermines the black male. In order to get some insight concerning this question, let us look first at Deborah and Esther, two women in the Bible, and the men associated with them."

Step 3—"For Such a Time as This"

Give a summary of the following:
Israelite society in biblical times was in every sense a strong, patriarchal society; it was one in which men normally made all of the important decisions and played such important roles as judge, warrior, and emissary to kings and other important government officials. Yet Barak specifically asked Deborah to go with him to raise an army and face the enemy (see Judges 4:8), and Mordecai begged Esther to intercede with the Persian king for her people (see Esther 4:8). Certainly the ancient Israelite men were as jealous of their male prerogatives as men are today, but they did not seem to see the exploits of Deborah and Esther as evidence that women had usurped the role that their husbands and brothers should have played. They included these narratives in their sacred literature because they showed, as nothing else could, that it was really God who saved the people and won their victories for them, and not the might of men trained in war or skilled in diplomacy.

These incidents and others showed the Israelite people that God was concerned about them and was with them in their struggles to survive and to obtain their rights. He could bring them to victory by working through one whom people supposed to be the weakest of instruments: a woman. This theme is shown again and again throughout the Bible, in 1 Samuel 2:4; Luke 1:52; and 1 Corinthians 1:27; as well as in the stories of Deborah and Esther.

Perhaps it is this great truth that God is trying to show us. Throughout black history in the U.S., black people, as a relatively powerless minority in a great, powerful nation, have had to trust in God because they had no other recourse. Yet God has been with blacks in their struggle, revealing this by insuring their survival and obtaining their rights for them through the seemingly least likely means: through their women.

Step 4—Prayer: Litany

With the members of the group giving the responses, recite the following litany:

O God, Creator, Redeemer, Sanctifier,
Have mercy on us.
For your love and continuing presence among us,
We thank you, O Lord.
For insuring our survival as a people and for being with us in our continuing struggle for liberation from all that would diminish our stature as human beings,
We thank you, O Lord.
For all men, women, and children who work for justice, liberation, and peace,
We thank you, O Lord.
That we may see you at work in our lives and history,
We pray to you, Lord God.
That we may join with Christ and with those who have gone before us to work for justice, liberation, and peace,

We pray to you, Lord God.
Glory to God whose power, working in us, can do infinitely more than we can ask or imagine; glory be to him from generation to generation in the church and in Christ Jesus for ever and ever.   *Amen.*
(cf. Ephesians 3:20-21)

Step 5—Activity: Dramatize "Oluronbi"

"Oluronbi" is a Yoruba cantefable (tale with a song) which attempts to explain why women have long hair. After giving the following background concerning the Yoruba, tell the tale, teach the song, and have the members of the group act out the story. In the song the person playing the tree spirit sings the "leader" parts, and everyone joins to sing the parts marked "chorus."

The Yoruba-speaking people live in the western part of Nigeria and the eastern part of the Republic of Benin. Since the ancestors of the present-day black Americans came from West Africa, some of them may have been Yoruba-speaking people.

In the evening, after the work is over, the Yoruba love to tell tales and act them out. Many of their tales are cantefables, i.e., tales with songs in them. During the day, many Yoruba are engaged in trading. They have many large outdoor markets where both men and women set up stalls and sell everything from food and clothing to radios and stereo sets. Although many Yoruba are now Christian or Moslem, traditionally they believed in many gods and spirits. The Yoruba believed that the gods or spirits would give them what they asked for if they sacrificed things such as sheep or goats or palm wine to them. Some of these gods or spirits were associated with specific hills or rocks or rivers or trees.

Most Yoruba are dark brown in color, but there are some light-skinned Yoruba who are described as "red" in color. They are said to be the same color of red as the oil which comes from the palm tree, which grows in the tropical rain forest or jungle where the Yoruba live. Giant mahogany trees also grow in this area.

Oluronbi

A certain mahogany tree was thought to have a very powerful spirit living inside it. People would stop in front of the tree on the way to their stalls in the market. They would promise to give the tree some sacrifice if it would make them successful in selling at the market. Most people promised a goat or a sheep.

One market woman, Oluronbi,[1] promised the mahogany tree spirit her only child if it would help her sell everything in record time. She sold all that she had for sale very quickly. But as she passed the tree on her way home, she remembered her promise and was horrified. She tried to hide, but the tree spirit began to sing to her a song (on the opposite page).

"I didn't make you promise your child," the spirit said. "You did it of your own free will."

Oluronbi rushed home. When she got there, she found that her daughter was already very sick. She snatched up the child, ran back to the mahogany tree, and tried to bargain with the spirit.

"I'll give you twenty sheep, a cow," she promised. The mahogany tree refused these offers and told her to consider her daughter already dead.

As the child began to sink into the ground, the mother held on tightly to her daughter's hair. The child's hair got longer and longer, and finally, she was saved. That is how women got long hair.

(Step 6—Evaluation)

To evaluate the session with members of the group, see the suggestions given in Appendix E.

---

[1] Oluronbi is pronounced "Oh-loo-ron-bee."

Leader
Ev-'ry-one prom-is es just one goat. Just one goat, a fine goat. Ev-'ry-one

prom-is-es one fine sheep. Just one sheep, coal black sheep. O-lu-ron-bi

prom-ised her on-ly child. Her own child, as red as palm oil. O-lu-ron-bi o,

jon-jo[2], Ma-hog-a-ny tree.

Session II

Our Bodies, the Temple of God

PURPOSE

To enable youth
- —to see themselves, souls and bodies, as the temple of God
- —to discuss the purposes of sex and the problems of sex abuse

OUTLINE OF SESSION

Step 1—Which Is Least Objectionable?
Step 2—The Temple of God
Step 3—Prayer: Litany
(Step 4—Evaluation)

Step 1—Which Is Least Objectionable?

1. Read to the group the following fantasy cast of characters:
- Harry, the eighteenth-century white slave owner who sneaks down to the slave cabins to sleep with Belle
- Belle, who encourages the master to have sex with her in order to obtain extra benefits for herself and for her children
- Dora, the "out for kicks" twentieth-century white girl who wants to have a black man, any black man, make love to her because she thinks black people know more about sex than white people do
- Jimmy, the twentieth-century black pimp with a "stable" of expensive girls who make more than enough for both them and him to live well
- Gina, a black prostitute who works for Jimmy and who hates men and gets her revenge by charging prices that no one would pay for any body

2. Have the members of the group choose which character they find least objectionable and explain why they have chosen that person.

3. Encourage members to give their ideas concerning the purposes of sex and the problems of sex abuse.

Step 2—The Temple of God

1. Have the youth turn to 1 Corinthians 3:16-17; 6:19; and Matthew 22:39.

2. Summarize the following comments.

For the Jews, the temple in Jerusalem was God's house. Although the Jews believed that God is everywhere, they believed that God was present in the temple in Jerusalem in a special way. The original architectural design of the temple was the same as the design used for a king's palace. When, at the dedication in the time of Solomon, the ark of the covenant was brought into the temple, the biblical writer tells us that a cloud, the sign of God's presence, filled the place (see 1 Kings 8:10-11). God's presence in the temple, and especially in the holy of holies, the innermost part of the temple, made it sacred, or consecrated, to God, and was a sign to the people that they had been especially chosen by God.

In the temple the holy of holies was separated from the people by a curtain. Only the Jewish high priest could enter this sacred area, and then only once a year, to atone for the sins of the people on the Day of Atonement. At the crucifixion of Jesus Christ the biblical writers tell us that the curtain which separated the people from the holy of holies split (Matthew 27:51). The separation of human beings from God had ended. Through Christ human beings are enabled to enjoy an enduring, growing, intimate relationship with God. Paul describes this relationship by saying that each Christian and each Christian gathering have become like the temple, consecrated to God, with the Spirit of God, the Holy Spirit, now dwelling in and among God's people.

Although the crucifixion and resurrection of Jesus Christ and the coming of the Holy Spirit broke down the barriers which had prevented human beings from enjoying an intimate, enduring, growing relationship of love with God and with one another, we still have not realized this ideal condition in its fullness. In practice, most of us find that we develop within a lifetime only a few special relationships with others where we feel free to be ourselves totally, to share our most secret dreams and ideas, or to cry openly if we so desire. Most of us instinctively know that such intimacy can and should take place only within those few long-lasting human relationships where we know that we are loved and accepted and where we feel that we can trust the other person totally. Such human relationships, in fact, mirror the relationship which exists between God and human beings.

What is true for emotional and intellectual intimacy is, of course, true for physical intimacy as well. Sex is a good gift of God not only for procreation but for enhancing and expressing that sort of total intimacy and love which grows and develops in a stable, long-lasting relationship. Casual sexual encounters do not and cannot express this kind of love. And in sexual relations used as a means to obtain money or other benefits, we do not love others as we love ourselves. Such relationships are actually unloving, since they reduce the other person to something less than human in using him or her as an object.

Marriage is a setting in which an enduring, intimate love can grow and develop. That is why sexual intimacy is seen to have a natural place in a marriage relationship. It is also why marriage is used as an image of the faithful, enduring, ever-growing relationship which should exist between God and the people of God (see the Book of Hosea; 2 Corinthians 11:1-2; Revelation 21:9-27). As Christians, we are committed to loving God with all our heart, soul, and mind. Because our bodies as well as our hearts, souls, and minds are consecrated to God, the use of our bodies in physical intimacy should take place within the same sort of faithful, enduring relationship to which we as Christians have committed our hearts, souls, and minds.

Step 3—Prayer: Litany

With the members of the group giving the responses, recite the following litany:

O God, Creator, Redeemer, Sanctifier,
Have mercy on us.

For loving and accepting us and for being One whom we can trust completely,
We thank you, O Lord.
For making it possible for us to enjoy an enduring, intimate, and growing relationship with you,
We thank you, O Lord.
For the good gift of sex, which serves as the expression of faithful, enduring human love and as the means of bringing new life into the world as a product of that love,
We thank you, O Lord.
That we may rightly use this gift and all your gifts to us,
We pray to you, Lord God.
May we always strive to love others with the love you showed us in your Son, Jesus Christ.
Amen.

(Step 4—Evaluation)

To evaluate the session with the group, see the suggestions given in Appendix E.

Appendixes

Appendix A

Outline of the Long-Term Project Model

I. Exposure to part of God's revelation on the theme to be considered (see "God's Revelation" in the long-term project outlines)

II. Initial response
   A. Commitment to join with other Christians to pursue the subject together
   B. Questions concerning God's revelation and the nature of your response, given the situation in which the group finds itself (see "Our Response" in the long-term project outlines), answered by:
      1. Study and research which should present other parts of God's revelation on the subject and help you to discover and analyze what the conditions in your area are in relation to the theme. (This aspect can be carried out both in the sessions themselves and during the planning for the social action project.)
      2. Planning, with prayer and the background of your research, to take some action which would bring the actual conditions closer to the ideal which God wills. (This action would continue the work of Christ in the world, which is what the church, the body of Christ, should do.)

III. Second response—Worship (for example, Eucharist or Holy Communion)
   A. Service of the Word
      1. Presents God's revelation on the theme discovered through study and prayer (II, B, 1, 2, above)
      2. May present the existing conditions discovered through study and research (II, B, 1, above)
   B. Communion
      1. Offering of the social action planned in union with Christ's offering of himself, as an extension of his work in the world
      2. Communing with Christ, the Head, and other members of his body to receive strength, grace, etc., to carry out his work

IV. Third response
   A. Carrying out with prayer the social action planned
   B. Revision—if original analysis of the problem, planning, execution, etc., proves faulty

V. Fourth response
   A. Evaluation to determine whether the social action undertaken to move conditions more toward those which God wills was successful; if not, why not?
   B. Evaluation to determine what was learned about the theme from the action taken, which might:
      1. Cause the group members to analyze the existing conditions in their locale in a different way than had been done in the initial response (II, B, 1, above)
      2. Cause the group members to see parts of God's revelation in a different light
      3. Cause the group members to choose another strategy for effecting change

VI. Possible fifth responses, which grow out of the evaluation (V, B, above)
   A. Pursue additional study and prayer concerning the revelation in order to discover deeper, additional, or different understandings which might be expressed in some form of planned social action
   B. Plan with additional research and prayer another strategy to try to bring about the change which was unsuccessful or only partially achieved in IV above
   C. Use the additional knowledge of the theme which was gained in the social action project to plan, research, and carry out a new social action project intended to solve another specific problem on the same general theme
   D. Undertake another theme for a project

Meditation Picture

"Left Back": A Simulation Game

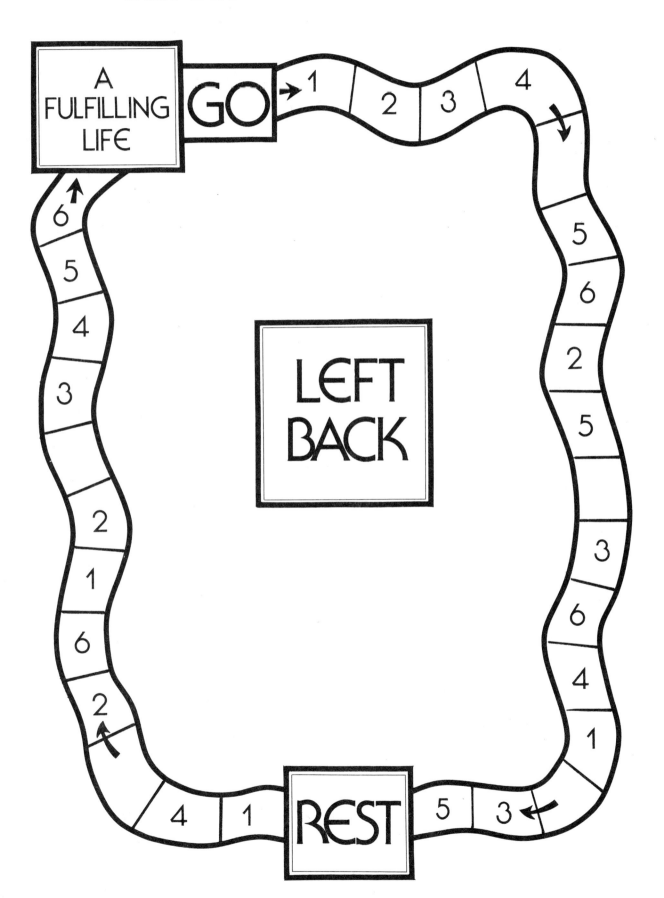

1. GETTING A JOB

- Ask a friend to help who is working in an area in which you are interested.
- Don't bother to search now because everyone says there are no jobs out there.
- Go to an employment agency.
- Ask at every store on Main Street.
- Search the want ads.

GREEN

3. CHILD REARING

- Teach your children to work hard.
- Explain to your children the consequences of their actions.
- Tell your children to shut up when they ask questions and you are busy.
- Beat your children whenever they do something wrong.
- Guide your children to make choices for themselves.

GREEN

5. HOUSING

- Move in with your aunt and her six children.
- Get what you like and worry about the price later.
- Buy or rent within your means.
- Rent and set up a plan to save toward a goal of purchasing.
- Use the GI Bill for purchasing a home.

GREEN

2. MARRIAGE

- Marry someone with money.
- Marry the first person who asks you.
- Marry someone with whom you can build a good future.
- Marry someone you love.
- Marry an older person with a steady job.

GREEN

4. FINANCIAL SECURITY

- Play the numbers.
- Invest in growth stocks.
- Invest in rental property.
- Push dope until you get ahead.
- Save 10 percent of each paycheck.

GREEN

6. EDUCATION

- Discipline yourself to study on your own.
- Get as much as you need in order to do what you want to do.
- Teach your children to value education.
- Keep a "C" average; you'll get through and have fun, too.
- Don't worry about education; making money is where it's at.

GREEN

1. GETTING A JOB

- Go to an employment agency—ADVANCE 5
- Search the want ads—ADVANCE 4
- Ask a friend to help who is working in an area in which you are interested—ADVANCE 2
- Ask at every store on Main Street—STAY WHERE YOU ARE
- Don't bother to search now because everyone says there are no jobs out there—GO BACK 1

BLUE

3. CHILD REARING

- Explain to your children the consequences of their actions—ADVANCE 5
- Guide your children to make choices for themselves—ADVANCE 5
- Teach your children to work hard—ADVANCE 4
- Tell your children to shut up when they ask questions and you are busy—STAY WHERE YOU ARE
- Beat your children whenever they do something wrong—GO BACK 1

BLUE

5. HOUSING

- Buy or rent within your means—ADVANCE 5
- Use the GI Bill for purchasing a home—ADVANCE 3
- Rent and set up a plan to save toward a goal of purchasing—ADVANCE 2
- Get what you like and worry about the price later—STAY WHERE YOU ARE
- Move in with your aunt and her six children—GO BACK 1

BLUE

2. MARRIAGE

- Marry someone with whom you can build a good future—ADVANCE 5
- Marry someone you love—ADVANCE 4
- Marry someone with money—ADVANCE 2
- Marry an older person with a steady job—ADVANCE 1
- Marry the first person who asks you—GO BACK 1

BLUE

4. FINANCIAL SECURITY

- Invest in growth stocks—ADVANCE 4
- Invest in rental property—ADVANCE 4
- Save 10 percent of each paycheck—ADVANCE 3
- Play the numbers—STAY WHERE YOU ARE
- Push dope until you get ahead—GO BACK 2

BLUE

6. EDUCATION

- Get as much as you need in order to do what you want to do—ADVANCE 5
- Teach your children to value education—ADVANCE 4
- Discipline yourself to study on your own—ADVANCE 4
- Keep a "C" average; you'll get through and have fun, too—STAY WHERE YOU ARE
- Don't worry about education; making money is where it's at—GO BACK 1

BLUE

1. GETTING A JOB

- Ask at every store on Main Street.
- Don't bother to search now because everyone says there are no jobs out there.

RED

3. CHILD REARING

- Tell your children to shut up when they ask questions and you are busy.
- Beat your children whenever they do something wrong.

RED

5. HOUSING

- Move in with your aunt and her six children.
- Get what you like and worry about the price later.

RED

2. MARRIAGE

- Marry the first person who asks you.
- Marry an older person with a steady job.

RED

4. FINANCIAL SECURITY

- Push dope until you get ahead.
- Play the numbers.

RED

6. EDUCATION

- Keep a "C" average; you'll get through and have fun, too.
- Don't worry about education; making money is where it's at.

RED

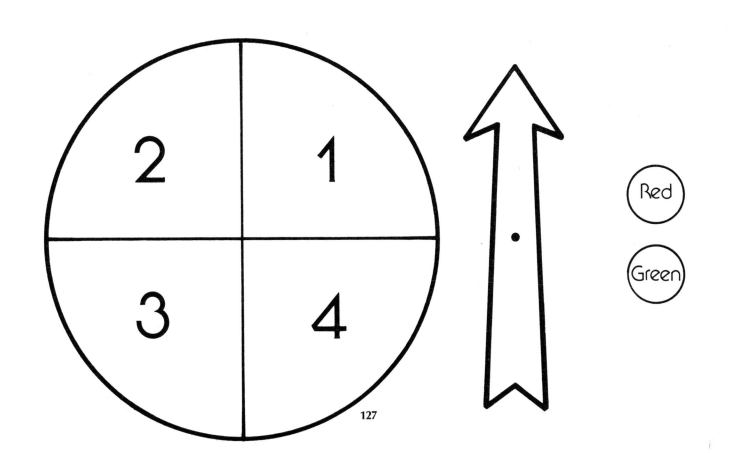

Additional Cards for "Dignity"

CHOICE

You are a black businessman. You have been asked to contribute to research on sickle-cell anemia. A representative from the research foundation says that sickle-cell anemia is a hereditary disease found only in black people in this country and that it is nearly always fatal. However, she says that a cure may be found through continued research.

CHOICE ONE: Do nothing and EVERYBODY GOES BACK TWO.

CHOICE TWO: Pay $100 to the bank and EVERYBODY GOES AHEAD TWO.

CHOICE

You have been asked to help out with a neighborhood breakfast program for school-age children.

CHOICE ONE: Refuse. STAY WHERE YOU ARE AND EVERYONE ELSE GOES BACK THREE.

CHOICE TWO: Volunteer to help twice a week. EVERYONE GOES AHEAD THREE.

-2 CUT THROAT

You are a ghetto landlord. For the fourth time you have refused your tenants' request to make plumbing repairs in an apartment house you own.

STAY WHERE YOU ARE AND EVERYBODY ELSE GOES BACK TWO.

-5

Your mother is elderly and cannot care for herself. You will have to quit your job to take care of her.

GO BACK FIVE.

+2

You are a teenager who has been looking for work for the last three months. You have become so discouraged that you have stopped looking. A church in your community has begun a program to help unemployed teenagers. GO AHEAD TWO.

TRAGEDY

PLAY THIS CARD ON YOUR NEXT MOVE

You have been disabled by a stroke. You are the sole support of your family of five. You will have to go on welfare. MOVE TO PUBLIC HOUSING.

-2

Your brother's rent is long overdue. He will have to pay $100 or be evicted. Pay $100 to the player of your choice and

GO BACK TWO.

CHOICE

Your church is joining with other churches in the city to provide and obtain funds to rehabilitate housing in your neighborhood.

You have been asked to serve on the steering committee.

CHOICE ONE: Refuse, and tell everyone else in the neighborhood that nothing will come from the work of the committee. EVERYONE GOES BACK TWO.

CHOICE TWO: Join the group. EVERYBODY GOES AHEAD TWO. LOSE ONE TURN FOR THE TIME IT TAKES.

CHOICE

You are black. A Puerto Rican group in the city has asked to join a coalition of black organizations working to bring pressure on unions and contractors in the construction industry to hire qualified workers regardless of race, color, or creed. You are a member of the committee which will consider the request of the Puerto Rican group.

CHOICE ONE: Vote to keep out the Puerto Rican group and urge other members of the committee to vote no on the grounds that the Puerto Ricans will get the jobs that blacks should have. EVERYBODY GOES BACK TWO.

CHOICE TWO: Vote to admit them. EVERYBODY GOES AHEAD TWO.

CHOICE

You are white and live in the suburbs. Your denomination has embarked on a fund-raising campaign to support a center to train clergy and laity as community organizers for the inner city. You have been asked to be chairperson for the campaign.

CHOICE ONE: Refuse on the grounds that the church should minister to the spiritual needs of the people and should not be involved in community organizing. STAY WHERE YOU ARE. EVERYBODY ELSE GOES BACK TWO.

CHOICE TWO: Agree to be chairperson. EVERYBODY GOES AHEAD TWO.

CHOICE

Your church committee on local hunger has asked you to research for them information concerning food stamps: who is eligible for them, where they are available, and how one goes about getting them.

CHOICE ONE: You refuse to do the job and tell everyone you know that people who use food stamps are "ripping off" the system. STAY WHERE YOU ARE. EVERYBODY ELSE GOES BACK TWO.

CHOICE TWO: You find the information, write it out and duplicate it, and send a copy to all the local congregations. EVERYBODY GOES AHEAD TWO. LOSE ONE TURN FOR THE TIME IT TAKES.

−5 EVERYBODY

Affirmative action programs at the new local university have been suspended because the administration has determined that the university never discriminated against anyone and, under the Bakke decision, does not need to maintain an affirmative action program.

EVERYBODY GOES BACK FIVE.

+5

You are elderly and find it difficult to get out to the grocery. Meals on Wheels has just started service in your neighborhood and will include you on its list.

GO AHEAD FIVE

CHOICE

You own a modest home and have been working two jobs to make ends meet. On election day there is a statewide proposition on the ballot which, if passed, would lower your property taxes but would also cut back services available to those on welfare.

CHOICE ONE: You vote for passage of the proposition and urge all your friends to vote for it because you think they ought to get all those people off the welfare rolls and make them work. STAY WHERE YOU ARE. EVERYBODY ELSE GOES BACK TWO.

CHOICE TWO: You vote against the measure. EVERYBODY GOES AHEAD TWO.

CHOICE

You have been asked to organize a letter-writing campaign to state legislators urging passage of the amendment granting residents of Washington, D.C., the right to elect representatives to Congress. Since the population of the District of Columbia is largely black, it is likely that members of Congress and senators elected there will be black.

CHOICE ONE: Refuse to help in the campaign and call for the defeat of the amendment because there are enough blacks in Congress. EVERYBODY GOES BACK TWO.

CHOICE TWO: Organize the letter-writing campaign and work to have a spokesperson for the amendment interviewed on TV. EVERYBODY GOES AHEAD TWO. LOSE ONE TURN FOR THE TIME IT TAKES.

+5 FREEDOM MOVE

You have begun organizing the people in your neighborhood to boycott grocery stores that sell spoiled meat and produce for the regular price.

GO AHEAD FIVE

FREEDOM MOVE

+5 EVERYBODY

The Black United Fund has just presented funds to your community for increased health care services.

EVERYBODY GOES AHEAD FIVE.

−5 CUT THROAT

You are a radio station executive. In return for increased advertising from one of the station's major sponsors, you have agreed to give an editorial describing American Indians as "more equal" than other Americans and calling for support for measures which have been introduced in Congress to abrogate all treaties made between the U.S. government and Indian tribes and to do away with off-reservation fishing and hunting rights which were guaranteed to the Indians.

STAY WHERE YOU ARE AND EVERYBODY ELSE GOES BACK FIVE.

Appendix E

Suggestions for Single-Session Evaluation with the Youth

Evaluation is an important part of an ongoing program. Only by getting an accurate assessment of what actually was learned in a session, what was liked and what was disliked, can the leaders hope to plan future sessions which will be interesting and productive for their particular group.

Below are some suggested questions for evaluating a session with the members of the youth group.

1. What did members of the group get from the session? What learnings took place?

2. Were the purposes listed at the beginning of the session achieved? What indications do you have that they were or were not achieved? If they were not achieved, why is that so? Were materials or instructions unclear? Planning or preparation of the leader(s) inadequate? Did the group find the session dull? Too complex? Too juvenile? Too far from their situation?

3. Which parts of the session did the group find most interesting? Why? Which were least interesting? Why?

4. Which sorts of things used in this session would members of the group like to see in other sessions?

Appendix F

A Suggested Commitment Service

Each of the long-term projects presented in this book assumes that the group will set aside an extended period of time for study, prayer, worship, and social action centered on a single theme or topic. Beginning the long-term project with a commitment service provides an opportunity for the members of the group to covenant with God and with one another to go through this experience together. The commitment service itself can take place as a short prelude to the first session, or it could be a more elaborate corporate communion. "A Form of Commitment to Christian Service," on pages 420 and 421 of *The Book of Common Prayer* can be used for this purpose. The service should include a summary of what the unit is about, such as the summary given in the background notes at the beginning of the unit, and some statement or statements which show that the youth are willing to undertake the project. The statement or statements can be simply presented by the youth in their own words, or, if "A Form of Commitment to Christian Service" is used, the statement, which in the commitment service is to precede the material given on pages 420 and 421, can take this form:

MINISTER: What do you wish?

LEADERS AND MEMBERS OF THE GROUP: We wish to join together for study, work, and prayer on *(name or description of unit)*.

A representative of the group then gives the summary of the unit, followed by a reaffirmation of baptismal promises, as given on page 303 or pages 292-294 in *The Book of Common Prayer*. Continue with "A Form of Commitment to Christian Service."

Be sure to have the group make preparations for the service in consultation with the person who will lead it.

Appendix G

Suggestions for Social Action Project Planning

Planning and carrying out a social action project on a given theme can be a very important part of our response to the will of God as revealed to us through our study and prayer. Although some social action projects can, perhaps, be planned entirely in one session, many will require some preliminary planning and then a period of time for researching and gathering information before definitive planning can take place. There are many possible procedures for planning a social action project. The following is one possible procedure for this planning. One of the suggested projects in the unit on Community is used to illustrate how the various steps in the procedure can be used. Before the group begins to plan the social action project, it may be useful to read through the long-term project outline in the unit to help generate ideas. It may also be helpful to review the explanation concerning the long-term project given in Appendix A.

A PROCEDURE FOR PLANNING THE SOCIAL ACTION PROJECT

1. Ask, "What are our problems as a group, as a community, as black people, etc., in the area with which this unit is concerned?" Then use the problems to determine what might be the goals (see Decision Making, Session II). Or "brainstorm" possible goals. (Brainstorming is a procedure in which members of a group spend a specified amount of time naming possible areas for consideration without interrupting the naming process to analyze any of the suggested possibilities.) Example: Problems—Suppose (a) the work done by the youth in Session I of the Community unit showed that there seemed to be few close or meaningful ties between the youth and the elderly in the congregation, and (b) the survey in Session III showed that people in the community surrounding the church felt that their children needed an educational system which would enable them to get jobs. Example: Possible goals for a social action project in the Community unit:

a. To help the people of the community surrounding the church building to work toward obtaining an educational system which would prepare their children to get jobs when they finish their education.

b. To develop closer, more meaningful ties between the youth and the elderly in the congregation and community.

2. Test the possible goals to help determine which one the group should attempt to reach (see "Some Questions for Testing Alternatives for a Project Goal" below). Example: The group decides that they are too few in number and do not have the necessary expertise to undertake goal a, which might involve organizing the community to pressure local and state educational authorities to make available training which would suit the needs of the community.

3. Formulate the goal to be reached. Example: Goal for a social action project in the Community unit—To develop closer, more meaningful ties between the youth and the elderly in the congregation and community.

4. Brainstorm possible alternative strategies for reaching the goal. Example: Some possible strategies for reaching the goal named in #3 above are: (a) to institute an interchange between elderly shut-ins and the youth, where the shut-ins would make quiet games for youth recreational programs and the youth would visit the elderly with accounts, pictures, etc., of events which have taken place in the church, community, or city; (b) to institute a substitute grandparent program in which youth would choose senior citizens as substitute grandparents and enjoy visits, meals, trips, etc., with them. (Research in the form of a survey showed that the congregation and community were interested in both strategies.)

5. Test the possible strategies to determine which one(s) the group will use (see "Some Questions for Testing Alternative Strategies" below). Example: The group decides that (a) in #4 above would be of great importance for extending and enhancing a sense of Christian community at this time.

6. Formulate the strategy (or strategies) to be used. Example: Strategy for reaching the goal formulated in #3 above: Institute an interchange between elderly shut-ins and the youth.

7. What tasks are part of the strategy? Each task becomes an objective to be accomplished in order to reach the goal. Example: Tasks which are part of the strategy formulated in #6 above are the following:

• Go to church, community, and city events of interest to the shut-ins and take pictures, save programs, etc.

• Survey shut-ins to determine which ones want to be included in interchange program and which events they especially want the youth to attend and share with them.

• Survey youth to determine which quiet games the

youth prefer how many sets would be necessary, etc.

• Contact youth who have used the games to prepare to visit and discuss games with shut-ins.

• Contact those who have attended and recorded the events to prepare for visits with shut-ins.

• Contact shut-ins to prepare for youth visits.

• Determine availability of cameras, etc.

• Purchase materials for scrapbooks, etc.

• Purchase materials for shut-ins to make games and deliver them.

• Get from shut-ins lists of materials needed for games to be made.

• Make scrapbooks, slide shows, etc.

8. Put the objectives in the order in which they must be accomplished, set a date when each should be completed, and assign or have people volunteer to accept responsibility for accomplishing them. Example (from tasks in #7 above):

• By January 15 a survey of shut-ins will be carried out to determine.... (Bob and Janice)

• By January 15 a survey of youth will be carried out to determine.... (Bob and Janice)

• By January 22 a list of materials will have been obtained.... (Loreen and Petey)

• By January 22 the availability of cameras, etc., for use at events.... (Bob and Janice)

• By January 29 materials for shut-ins to make games.... (Loreen and Petey)

• Between January 15 and March 31 members of the group will visit events of interest to shut-ins.... (Jay, Hashina, Tafitti, Larry, Butch)

• By March 31 materials for making scrapbooks, etc., will be purchased.... (Hashina and Larry)

• By April 15 members of group will have made scrapbooks, etc.... (Hashina and Larry with others)

• By April 20 all involved will have been contacted for first visits to shut-ins. (Bob and Janice)

• Week of April 22-29 first visits to shut-ins ... (Loreen, Petey, Jay, Hashina, Tafitti, Larry, Butch, other youth in community)

SOME QUESTIONS FOR TESTING ALTERNATIVES FOR A PROJECT GOAL

1. Which area do we value most? Which area is of such importance to us that we would like to see immediate changes take place?

2. Is it possible that a group such as ours could attack this problem area successfully? What are the facts for and against? What are our assets and limitations with regard to this area? (Assets and limitations should include not only tangible things but also intangibles, such as the feelings of the members of the group concerning the proposed area for concern and the types of experiences one might have in working in it. Where it is difficult to decide whether or not the group could attack the problem successfully and reach the goal, the use of force-field analysis, as shown in Session III in the Decision Making unit, might prove useful.)

3. Is it possible that we would be wasting our efforts working in this area because adequate work is already being done in that area, because it seems unlikely that change could occur there in the near future, or for some other reason? What are the facts for and against our working in this area?

4. What might be the consequences if our group chose to work in this area? Is it possible that there might be some unpleasant consequences for the group or for individual members of the group or for others? If so, are we (or the persons who would be affected) willing to live with the unpleasant consequences?

5. Why are we choosing to work in this area? Is it to bring about more loving or just conditions, or is it to gain revenge, punish someone, or whatever?

SOME QUESTIONS FOR TESTING ALTERNATIVE STRATEGIES

1. Which strategy accords best with our values, especially our Christian values?

2. Can a group such as ours use this strategy successfully? Do we have enough people, time, expert knowledge (if called for), etc.?

3. What might be the consequences if our group chose to use this strategy? Is it possible that there might be some unpleasant consequences for the group, for individual members of the group, or for others? If so, are we (or the persons who would be affected) willing to live with the unpleasant consequences?

Appendix H

Coping with Negative Aspects in a Social Action Project

There are likely to be some negative aspects involved in any social action project which is planned. A major step toward dealing with these negatives involves admitting and being aware that they exist. This step should take place during the discussions of limitations and consequences which would take place during project planning. (See Appendix G.) Negative aspects may come about as a consequence of the goal decided upon or of the strategy chosen to reach the goal. Or they may result from limitations which the group has with regard to the goal area. However they come about, these aspects of the social action project can prevent the group from reaching its goal if such aspects are not examined and dealt with before work on the social action project actually begins. Below are some suggestions for coping with negative aspects of the social action project.

1. *Accept those limitations which cannot be changed.* If work on the social action project is to be effective, it must be preceded by a frank acknowledgment of the possible limitations which the group might face. Some of these limitations may involve tangible things. For example, in the social action project outlined in Appendix G, lack of money to buy the various supplies needed and lack of photographic equipment are tangible things which the group might see as possible limitations. However, it is the less obvious limitations, in the form of attitudes and feelings present in members of the group or in those with whom they will be interacting, which are more likely to remain hidden from view.

Bringing these out for discussion involves real penance, in the sense of turning toward what we would rather turn away from, and confession, in the sense of acknowledging what needs to be changed. Thus, for example in the social action project outlined in Appendix G, some members of the group may be frightened of or dislike interacting with sick or shut-in persons, and some chronically ill shut-ins may be "cranky" and very difficult company for the youth. Potential limitations of this kind must also be dealt with if they are not to jeopardize the success of the social action project.

It is sometimes possible to work out strategies for neutralizing some of these limitations (see #2 below). However, it often happens that all of the limitations cannot be neutralized. It is unlikely, for example, that the members of the group can do much to change a "cranky," hostile, elderly shut-in into a person with whom it is less difficult to interact. Limitations which cannot be changed will just have to be acknowledged and accepted along with the pleasant experiences which will result from the project. Or if they seem to be an obstacle for many members of the group, another social action project should be considered.

2. *Accept the assets: discuss the positive reasons for choosing a particular social action project or goal.* This sort of discussion often makes the unpleasant or negative aspects bearable. Example from the social action project outlined in Appendix G: Elderly shut-ins must often feel totally cut off not only from the youth but also from the entire community. Since the youth are able to get around and attend events which the shut-in cannot attend, the youth are able to relieve in some measure the loneliness of the shut-in. On the other hand, since shut-ins often find that they have little to do to fill up the time, they might enjoy making games which the youth could use in recreation programs. These are assets and positive reasons for choosing the goal.

3. *Build in strategies to eliminate potentially negative aspects.* In some cases something can be built into the social action project which would eliminate the possibility that certain negative aspects will occur. Example: If lack of money and equipment might hinder the group in carrying out the project outlined in Appendix G, plans for fund raising and for borrowing the necessary equipment can be built into the project. In the same project some of the youth might complain that visits to elderly shut-ins would be boring because some lonely shut-ins talk too long. Again, this is a potential negative which can, perhaps, be eliminated. Each shut-in could be told at the beginning of the visit that the group would like to make several visits that day and cannot stay for too long a time at any one place.

4. *Divide what must be done in the project into "frontline" jobs and "back-room" jobs.* Only those in "frontline" jobs would have to face the unpleasant situations, and only those who can cope with the unpleasant situations would perform the "frontline" jobs.

Example: In the project outlined in Appendix G, if there are some members of the group who are frightened of or dislike interacting with shut-in persons, they could be given jobs which do not involve direct contact with shut-ins (for example, the jobs assigned to Bob and Janice in the section "A Procedure for Planning the Social Action Project," Step 8, in Appendix G). These are "back-room" jobs. Of course, if there are more people willing to take "back-room" jobs than "frontline" ones, then another social action project would probably be more appropriate for the group than the one chosen. It is important, also, that those who carry out "frontline" jobs not belittle those who do the "back-room" jobs. Both kinds of tasks are important for the success of the project.

5. *Assign several people to a task that might "overawe" or frighten one person or which might seem unpleasant if he or she had to do it alone.* If necessary, enlist the support of an adult. Example: In the social action project outlined in Appendix G, actually visiting the shut-ins is a task which a single member of the group might find frightening. Thus, several persons could plan to visit together.

Even when one person is assigned a task, support and encouragement from the group are very helpful, especially when he or she runs into difficulties.

6. *Role-play anticipated difficulty situations and follow the role play with a discussion of the probable feelings of all those involved.* Examples of role play followed by discussion are found in the unit on Suffering, Election, and Mission, Session II, Step 1 (Alternative B), and in many other outlines.

Appendix I

A Form for Home Devotions

In each long-term project it is suggested that the youth put together individual devotional programs which they can use mornings, afternoons, or evenings during the time when they are at work on the social action part of the project and afterward, if they wish. These home devotions are meant to help the members of the group remain in close contact with Christ so that what they think and do during this part of the project is rooted in him. The form suggested here is based on "Daily Devotions for Individuals and Families," pages 137-140 in *The Book of Common Prayer*. Have each person fill in the various parts of the form with Bible verses, prayers, etc., which are appropriate for the theme of the unit and which have some meaning for him or her.

OPENING VERSE

A short Bible verse or line from a hymn can be used to recall the unit theme. Have each person choose several verses which are appropriate. These can be changed occasionally in order to give variety to the devotions.

READING

A longer scriptural passage than the opening verse can be used here. Again, if several appropriate passages are chosen, they can be changed occasionally for variety. Encourage the youth to take time after they have read the passage to reflect on it.

HYMN OR CANTICLE; APOSTLES' CREED

Optional. Canticles are found on pages 47-53 and pages 85-96 of *The Book of Common Prayer*, and the Apostles' Creed is on pages 53 and 96. Saying the Apostles' Creed provides an opportunity for reaffirma-tion of faith, which is always appropriate in a daily devotional program.

PRAYERS FOR OURSELVES AND OTHERS; PRAYERS OF THANKSGIVING AND PENITENCE

These prayers can be quite simple, such as "For Jerry, who is discouraged," or "Thank you, Lord, for guiding us in this venture." The youth can include in this section prayers for continued help and guidance in carrying out the social action project and for the people involved in it, prayers for forgiveness when the youth fall short, and thanksgiving prayers for any successes or achievements which occur, as well as prayers for their own lives and the lives of ones close to them.

THE LORD'S PRAYER

THE COLLECT

Optional. Some youth may want to include in their daily devotions a prayer which will "collect" many of the ideas that the group has discussed and present them all to God. A collect is a prayer that does just that. Collects and prayers appropriate for the theme of the unit are suggested in the "Home Devotions" section in each long-term project.

CLOSING VERSES

A short verse of praise, thanksgiving, or benediction can close the devotions.

After they have decided on the materials to be included in the devotional program and have written them out, have the youth staple the sheets together to form booklets which can be used at home. Attractive covers for the booklets can be made from construction paper and decorated with designs and symbols which are appropriate for the theme of the unit.

Appendix J

The Use of Religious Celebration in the Long-Term Project

In each unit where there is a long-term project outline, it is suggested that the youth plan and carry out a religious celebration based on the theme of the project. One possible celebration would be a Eucharist, or Holy Communion, service based on "An Order for Celebrating the Holy Eucharist" in *The Book of Common Prayer,* pages 400ff. This service would be planned jointly by the youth and the minister. Some suggestions of possibilities for each part of this Order are given in the second section below. The following has been written with the celebration of the Eucharist in mind, but groups can easily adapt this for their usual order of service.

In worship we acknowledge God as the only Person, cause, or thing worth giving ourselves wholly to. This acknowledgment of the supreme worth of God and presentation of ourselves can take place when we give ourselves to study and prayer to discover the will of God and to equip ourselves to do it. It can take place when we give ourselves to prayer and work directed toward doing God's will. It can take place in ritualistic ways. It takes place especially at the Eucharist, or Communion. One purpose of this service used as a part of the long-term project, then, would be to make clear that all that has been done in the unit and all that will be carried out after the celebration is, in a sense, worship.

At this service we first study the word of God. Thus, the first part of the service ("Gather in the Lord's Name" and "Proclaim and Respond to the Word of God" in *The Book of Common Prayer*) can include some of the Bible passages, prayer, study, and discussion which was presented earlier in the unit.

In the second part of the service, as we bring our gifts and ourselves to the altar and receive the bread and wine, we express symbolically our intention to give ourselves in our daily lives to the will of God, as we have come to understand it through our study.

It was Jesus Christ who gave himself most fully to carry out the will of God. In the service of Communion we celebrate the re-presentation of Christ's offering. His work to carry out the will of God goes on in the world through what Paul calls his Body, the church. As members of the church, we are all mystically part of Christ's Body, and his work is carried on through us. The gifts which are brought forward at the offertory— the money and the bread and wine—are symbols and expressions of ourselves, our time, talent, and resources which we offer to God. Thus, at every Eucharist, or Holy Communion as members of Christ's Body, we bring ourselves and our work to be offered in and with Christ, the Head of the Body, for his ministry in the world. In the service used with the long-term project, which will conclude the study-prayer part of the unit and usher in that portion which is oriented toward action and prayer, the major offering to be brought and offered in and with Christ for his ministry is the social action project which has been planned.

In making decisions concerning the social action project and in planning it, the youth implicitly acknowledged and responded to the God revealed in Holy Scripture. By their decisions they freely undertook to join with Christ in his ministry. Now they come to acting out this decision, first in the worship celebration and then in carrying out the project.

It is vitally important that, as humans, we act out our decisions in symbolic ways; we are then committed to them and can carry on with life with a definite sense of where we are going and what we are about to do. That is, in fact, a major reason why, even though all of our life should be essentially worship, we set aside times for formal worship services. Formal worship makes explicit what is less clearly expressed in all that we do in our lives as Christians. Every Eucharist or Communion service, then, is an opportunity for clarifying who we are as Christians and why we are doing what we do. Although there will be brought to this service particular decisions about a particular task, at every worship service we are, in fact, renewing and making clear again our decision to join with Christ in his ministry of reconciling the world to God and bringing to fruition God's kingdom of love, peace, justice, freedom, and joy.

SOME SUGGESTIONS FOR PLANNING A EUCHARIST USING "AN ORDER FOR CELEBRATING THE HOLY EUCHARIST" (IN THE BOOK OF COMMON PRAYER, pages 400ff.)

Gather in the Lord's Name

Ancient people thought that a name told something about its owner's personality or nature. What has been said about the Lord's name (or nature) in the unit? Gathering in the Lord's name might include any of the suggestions listed below:

- Bible verses which incorporate some of what has

been discussed concerning God and which would help everyone realize that they are in the presence of God.

- A silent or directed meditation taken from those used during the unit.
- Visual aids for use with meditation.

Proclaim and Respond to the Word of God
Proclamation

Required: A Gospel passage (use one with some bearing on the theme). Proclaim the Word of God as expressed in the unit through a talk or readings, drama, slide show, song, dance, or other art form or a combination of these forms.

Possible Responses

- Confession. Once faced with the Word of God, we realize that we have fallen short. If the group wishes to write a special confession for this occasion, they can be guided by the confessions on pages 41, 79, and 127 of *The Book of Common Prayer*. After confession, there is an absolution or an assurance of God's forgiveness. The Peace may follow the confession and absolution, or assurance, of God's forgiveness. The Peace then becomes a symbol of the reconciliation which takes place after we have acknowledged our sin and received forgiveness.

- The Creed or other statement of our belief. By repeating together a statement of our belief, we show that we believe the Word which has been proclaimed to us.

- A resolution to act in accord with the Word that has been proclaimed is another possible response. The resolution or resolutions could be an explanation or description of the project or projects which have been planned in response to God's Word. Visual aids (slides, posters, buttons, etc.) can also be used to make the presentations more vivid and more easily understood.

Pray for the World and the Church

In this prayer we offer the world and the church through Christ to God to be reconciled to him and transformed by him into the community of love, justice, peace, and joy which God wills. In this service prayers can be offered especially for those who are part of the youth group and for all those involved in the project being undertaken, that they may both be transformed themselves and be united with Christ in his reconciling, transforming ministry.

Often, the prayer for the world and the church provides for responses by the entire congregation. By giving the response, then, everyone in the entire congregation joins in presenting the petitions. Time is often set aside, also, for those present to add either silently or aloud their own petitions, intercessions, and thanksgivings. The prayers on pages 383-393 of *The Book of Common Prayer* can serve as a model if members of your group would like to write their own prayer for the world and the church.

Prepare the Table

The major offering at this service is the life and work of those who have committed themselves to work in the project which has been outlined. Since the bread and wine at the service represent the gift of ourselves, it would be fitting for those who will be offering themselves in this service to make or buy the bread and wine. If money is needed to carry out the projects, it would be appropriate for it to be presented at this service. Symbols or pictures of the planned projects and of the part that various participants will play in them can also be presented. An offertory procession can be used to bring to the altar all the gifts.

Make Eucharist

Eucharistic prayers can be chosen from any given in Rite One (pages 333-336), Rite Two (pages 361-364, 367-376), or on pages 402-405 of *The Book of Common Prayer*. The Eucharistic prayer should be chosen in consultation with the priest who is the celebrant for this Eucharist or the leader involved in the Communion service.

Break the Bread
Share the Gifts of God

(If you wish, a blessing and/or dismissal can be used to conclude the service. See pages 339 and 340 or 366 of *The Book of Common Prayer*.)

Special vestments for the participants and for the altar add greatly to the effectiveness of this special celebration and to transmitting or recalling its message. Banners can also be used in procession or hung on the walls. Suggestions for making vestments and banners are found in Appendix N.

Music can be used in many places in the service. The service can open and close with music; music can be used in processions, between parts of the service, and during Communion, as well as be a part of the proclamation of or response to the Word of God.

Appendix K

Suggestions for Mid-Project Revision

Mid-project revision can take place whenever there is a need for those working on the social action project to revise strategies or sort through unresolved feelings. It can be called for by either the adult leaders or by members of the group. Those who have felt the need for such a session might act as leaders, relating the events or incidents which led them to assemble the group for this purpose.

After everyone knows why the session was called, the group can, if they wish, during a period of silence bring the problem in their minds to Christ, as they have done in many of the prayers in the outlined sessions. Problem events or incidents can be role-played and/or discussed in order to determine what actually is happening and how crippling feelings can be resolved and things made better. Or any of the other techniques listed in Appendix H, "Coping with Negative Aspects in a Social Action Project," can be used in this exercise.

Appendix L

Suggestions for Project Evaluation

After the social action portion of the long-term project has run a specified period of time, whether you wish to continue it or not, it is best to have an evaluation. Evaluation can be useful (a) for analyzing and assessing what actually took place in the unit, (b) for determining how things could have been done better, (c) to discover what learnings took place in the action part, (d) in order to be able to use the learnings from this project in carrying out other projects on the theme. Some possible questions for such an evaluation are:

1. Did the study-prayer part of the unit, given in the outlined sessions, provide an adequate background for understanding the unit theme? God's revelation concerning it? Its relationship to the peculiar circumstances of black American Christians?

2. Did the celebration serve to bring into focus what was happening in the study-prayer and prayer-action parts of the long-term project? How these parts can relate to one another? How we can relate to God and to one another with reference to this theme? If not, how could it have been made to serve these functions?

3. Did the study-prayer portion of the long-term project, the worship, the home devotions, and the mid-project revision session(s) provide adequate support for the social action part of the project? If not, how could they have been altered so as to provide this support?

4. Was the social action project successful? Did it achieve the goal? If not, did it fail to reach the goal because (a) of inadequate background given in the study-prayer part of the unit; (b) the strategy chosen was not really appropriate to reach the goal; (c) of inadequate planning; (d) of lack of interest or commitment on the part of members of the group; (e) members of the group had unacknowledged and unresolved feelings and attitudes involving the area chosen for work, which hindered the project; (f) members of the group were already too heavily involved in other activities to take on the responsibilities of the action project; (g) members of the group were too few to carry out the project as designed; or (h) of other reasons?

5. Does the action part of the project need to be continued for a longer period of time (a) to determine whether or not it will help effect change; (b) because it helps fill an important need; (c) for some other reason?

6. If it seems unlikely that the goal can be reached, should the project be abandoned, revamped extensively, or some other action taken?

7. What was learned about the unit theme in the social action part of the long-term project? Did the group discover ways other than the ones originally thought of for reaching the goal?

8. What other learnings (about self, about others, etc.) came out of the social action part of the project?

9. Did the attitudes or feelings of those in the group seem to influence the success or failure of the long-term project?

10. Did the entire long-term project—study, prayer, research, social action, and worship—help clarify how the members of the group can respond to God's revelation concerning the unit theme, given their particular circumstances?

Appendix M

Using a Retreat to Begin the Long-Term Project

A weekend retreat, youth conference, or "lock-in" can be used to carry out some of the work of the long-term project. After a short commitment service, the theme can be introduced by using two of the outlined sessions in the unit. Then the group can do some preliminary planning for the social action project (perhaps to the point of formulating a goal and positing two or three possible strategies for reaching the goal) and plan and carry out the religious celebration for the unit. Others of the outlined sessions can be presented, research and planning for the social action part of the project continued, possible negative aspects of the project dealt with, home devotions formulated, and revision(s) and evaluation carried out in sessions to take place after the retreat is over. A sample outline for such a retreat would look like this:

Friday Evening—Short Commitment Service and one of the outlined sessions in the unit.

Saturday Morning—Another of the outlined sessions in the unit.

Saturday Afternoon—Preliminary planning of the social action project and planning of the religious celebration for Sunday.

Saturday Evening—Relaxation (film, dance, etc.)

Sunday Morning—Celebration

Making Banners, Vestments, Booklet Covers, Etc.

Banners, vestments, covers for devotional booklets (see Appendix I), lapel buttons, and other visual aids decorated with designs, slogans, and symbols are especially useful in helping to transmit and recall the message of the unit. For the religious celebration in the project, the members of the group can make various decorations and other objects appropriate to their form of celebration. Banners can be used in processions or hung on the walls of the place where the celebration is held, and the participants can wear large lapel buttons displaying slogans or symbols which are appropriate for the unit. The devotional booklets which the youth have made can also be decorated in this way.

There are many possible choices of designs, slogans, or symbols for decoration. Banners and lapel buttons may display slogans based on the unit theme (for example, "Help Me Love Me" for the unit on Loving Ourselves, or "Play Fair" for the Justice unit, or "You've Got to Choose" for the unit on Decision Making). Vestments, booklet covers, and other visual aids can be decorated with symbols which are traditionally associated with the theme of the unit, such as balances for the unit on Justice, or sheaves of wheat or a loaf of bread for the Bread unit. Of course, traditional Christian symbols, such as the cross, the triangle (symbol of the Trinity), the circle (symbol of eternity), can also be used. Below are some traditional African designs which could also be drawn and traced on cloth or paper as decorations.